WELSH WIT AND HUMOUR

Welsh Wit and Humour

by

Byron Evans

First edition: 2001
New edition: 2008
© Text: Byron Evans

ISBN: 978-1-84524-111-7

Cover design: Sian Parri
Cover illustration: Dylan Williams
Cartoons: Siôn Amlyn

First published in 2001 by Gwasg Carreg Gwalch
12 Iard yr Orsaf, Llanrwst, Wales LL26 0EH
☎ 01492 642031   📠 01492 641502

New edition published in 2008 by Llygad Gwalch,
Ysgubor Plas, Llwyndyrys, Pwllheli, Gwynedd LL53 6NG
☎ 01758 750432   📠 01758 750438
✆ books@carreg-gwalch.com   Website: www.carreg-gwalch.com

Dedication: to my wife, Peg: born and bred in the rich choral and mining traditions of Dyfnant. Thanks for all her encouragement and practical help in the preparation of the text; and for the sound of her laughter as she did it!

Contents

A Kind of Humour

On the eve of the theological college scholarship entrance exam, five of us sat in the college common room, tense and full of apprehension. The door opened and a short, portly and bespectacled figure entered. The whole atmosphere changed as he approached with a wide grin and admonished us for looking so pathetic. He too was a candidate, but didn't seem to have a care in the world. Without further ado he took charge of the evening. Soon we were relaxed and laughing at his unending stock of stories and this lasted until we went to bed.

One of the many humorous tales he told us was about Twm and Dai, the sons of a local farmer. Twm was a farm labourer who had lost his eye in an incident on the farm. Dai, meanwhile, had applied for a scholarship to a theological college. The day before the scholarship examination Dai was in bed with a severe dose of flu'. After finishing his work, Twm went to sympathise with Dai and to offer a solution to his problem. He offered to go and sit the exam instead of him.

'Out of the question,' croaked Dai. 'You don't know the first thing about Bible studies!'

'Never mind about that,' was the reply. 'I'll get by and don't you worry.'

In spite of Dai's feeble protestations, Twm went off the next day to sit the exam, The Professor conducting the proceedings announced that the exam. Would be 'by signs only'. He went on to hold up one finger.

Twm, watching him closely through his good eye, held up two fingers.

The Professor then held up three fingers. Twm

responded angrily by holding up his fist.

Finally, the Professor produced an apple from his pocket and held it up. Twm put his hand in his pocket and brought out the sandwiches that his mother had given him.

The Professor returned to his colleagues and told them that there had been an outstanding student in the group that day.

'I held up one finger to indicate that there was only one God,' he said. 'But this student held up two fingers indicating the father and the Son.'

'I then tried him out by holding up three fingers suggesting that there might even be three gods or more. But he held up his fist to indicate that there was only one true God.'

'Finally, I produced an apple to remind him of God's Fall in the garden of Eden, but he produced the food his mother had given him, signifying that God had provided other foods for Adam, and he need not have eaten the apple and bring sin into the world.'

Twm returned home and told Dai it had been a 'right old doddle'.

'Just think,' Twm said. 'This old boy stood in front of us and held up one finger, telling me that I had only one eye. I soon put a stop to that caper by holding up two fingers! Then, would you believe it? He held up three fingers, showing me that he had two eyes and, but I only had one. So I shook my fist at him. But to cap it all, he went into his pocket and offered me an apple, if you please! But I showed him that our mum had taken care of me!'

The story was told with well-timed pauses, sharp eye movements behind the thick spectacles, elaborate hand movements and a modulated voice with a thick Welsh accent. The performance was one of many hilarious moments that night. In one of his more sober moments, he went on to claim that all great writers [which included himself, of course] communicated in a humorous way. His list also included Chaucer, Carlyle, Swift, Daniel Owen [who was his favourite Welsh writer], Sir Gwynne Jones and the author[s] of *Y Mabinogion*. According to him, all these writers conveyed their values through humour, but humour had to be more than the cause of mere laughter. The humorist had to be more than just a clown, although a certain amount of clowning is involved.

Humour, therefore, can include geniality, homeliness of speech, images drawn from everyday life, and even blunt eloquence: qualities which are used superbly in the fiction of 'Will Bryan and the Clock' from the book entitled 'Rhys Owen', written in Welsh by Daniel Owen [1836-95] and translated into English by D.M. Lloyd.

> 'You know that old eight-day clock in our kitchen? Of late it has been apt to lag a bit behind time, – *a fault by the way not unknown amongst other orders of superior beings* . . . I thought all along I could cure it if I had the time, although I had never before tried to clean a clock, – but you know that I am not bad at all at trying my hand at things! Well then, when the folks went to Wrexham Fair, – *with strict injunctions that Will in the meantime should diligently apply himself to weighing and wrapping sugar, which occupation the said Will considered unworthy of his admitted abilities, and the said Will, following his more congenial inclinations, betook himself to clock-cleaning, thinking that thereby he did not waste valuable time by putting the time-keeper to rights.*

But it is a bigger job than I reckoned, I tell you; for in taking it to pieces, I had to write notes where every part came from, and to what they belonged. And after I had cleaned it all, and put butter on every cog, screw and bar, – there was no oil in the house – it was well on in the afternoon, although I did without dinner so as not to waste time, and it was high time to start putting it together again before the gaffer came home from the fair. *So far – good*. But when I betook myself to putting the old eight-day piece together, and to consult my notes, – you never saw the like: I was like Mr. Brown, the vicar; I couldn't read my own notes! But I learnt this much, that the man who goes to clean clocks, just like the preacher, should be able to do the job without notes. You never saw such a mess. But you must remember that I was *labouring under great disadvantages*, for my only tools were a jack-knife and a pair of blacksmith's tongs. I was running with sweat, lest the old "Pilgrim's Progress" should return from the fair before I had assembled the old clock somehow. I worked like fury and got it together into some sort of shape. But I had one spare wheel, and not the remotest idea where to fix it or what to do with it, so I put it in my pocket, – here it is, look,'said Will, as he showed it to me.

'Well, I put the old "eight" back in its place , and wound it and the first thing that *"my nabs"* did was to strike and strike right to the bottom. It struck thousands and thousands, and the noise was driving me dotty; the din was such that I feared the neighbours would think that the squire's daughter was getting married! After striking all it could 'my nabs' decided to stay put. As long as I pushed the pendulum the old "eight" kept going fairly well, but as soon as I stopped so would the clock. To tell the truth, I laughed till I was rolling – I couldn't stop laughing to save my life. So here endeth a true account of the clock-cleaning.'

[The phrases in italics are in English in the original.]

• • •

But there are also other kinds of humour and one of these – unconscious humour – creates spontaneous amusement for us all, even laughter in the most unexpected places. Such a situation must have been experienced by those who passed a church in Denbighshire. Above the entrance was the inscription, THIS IS THE GATE TO HEAVEN'. Underneath it had been placed a notice: 'This gate will be closed for three months due to repair work'!

• • •

But the rapier-like humour of the great Welsh political speech-makers, like Aneurin Bevan and Lloyd George, has different qualities and intentions. Humour is not used merely to entertain, although it does this well enough, but to de-bunk, to defuse, sometimes even to destroy. Dependent on quick wits, a cool nerve and a superb command of language it is perhaps most forcibly felt in the repartee of the hustings. On one occasion, when Lloyd George was speaking on the theme of Welsh Independence a confident heckler from the crowd yelled 'And what about Hell?' To which Lloyd George's immediate riposte was 'Every man to his own country!'

Legends abound of the Welsh Wizard's linguistic prowess. In what must have been a brilliant recruiting speech at Bangor in 1915 he referred to 'lame ants', an intriguing and incongruous image; then he told his audience the old Welsh legend 'of a man who was given a series of what appeared to be impossible tasks to perform ere he could reach the desires of his heart. Amongst other things, he had to recover every grain of seed that had been sown in a large field, and bring them all in without one missing: by sunset. He came to an ant-hill and enlisted the sympathies of the industrious little creatures. They spread over the field and before sundown the seed was all in, except for one grain, and as the sun was setting over the western skies, a lame ant hobbled along with that final grain. Some of us have youth and vigour and suppleness of limb; some of us are crippled with years or infirmities, and we are at best but lame ants. But we can all limp along with some share of our country's burden, and thus help her in this terrible hour to win the desire of her heart.'

• • •

Family situations, often retold in autobiographical writings like 'Old Memories' by Sir Henry Jones [1852-1922], provide us with delightful glimpses of gently humorous situations shared initially by the participants but then, recognised as having the power to amuse and entertain a wider audience. The writer begins: ' I am tempted to tell another little story. It illustrates so well the atmosphere of our happy home. I was home on a visit, and, I believe a professor at St. Andrew's at the time. I was sitting in the kitchen, the only living room, chatting with my mother, when my father came in. He had been out, taking his usual evening walk after his day's work, along the quiet country road, and in the dark.

'I think,' he said to my mother as he was sitting down, 'I think that I have caught two lovers.'

'No!' cried my mother as full of interest as if she were a young woman, 'who were they, Elias?'

'I'll not tell you,' he replied, 'for you will not believe me.'

She begged, and of course, he gave in, bidding me observe that my mother would refuse to believe him.

'It was Robert Davies, the tailor,' he said, 'and Mrs. Roberts, the widow who lives at the chapel house.'

Robert Davies was a serious-minded elder, about sixty-five years old and a widower.

'Don't talk nonsense!' cried my mother, rejecting his tale just as he had foretold.

'Well,' said he at length, when she persisted in her unbelief, 'I'll tell you what I saw, and you can judge for yourself. As I was passing the door of Mrs. Roberts's house, it was opened and a flood of light poured out. Robert Davies walked in, and I saw him quite plainly. He had a ham under his arm. I lingered about, and in about a quarter of an hour or twenty minutes Robert Davies came out, *without the ham.*'

'Well! Well!' cried my mother, her scepticism completely overcome by the evidence of the "ham", which was evidently, for her as for my father, conclusive proof of marital intentions, if not also of tender passion. I thought the whole scene between my mother and my father one of the most humorous I had ever witnessed, and felt I had discovered a new use for hams!'

Of course, what we realise is that the subtle humour of this situation could only have been relayed by the individual who observed the incident sympathetically yet objectively, and had the skills of language to retell it without losing any of its intrinsic, gentle irony.

• • •

It is claimed that one of the functions of comedy is to exclude those who cannot or will not fit in to the harmonious social pattern: Malvolio is given as a prime example. But often, humour is inclusive in its intention, with the writer seeking the active participation of the reader to give the text a richer, more amusing quality than it would otherwise have. How can we read Dylan Thomas's 'Return Journey' without subscribing to the text all our own memories of youth and indiscretion! We read only one side of the conversation but there is not a reader who cannot provide, unerringly, the missing lines! His 'whistling after the girls' interlude invites from us all, and from Swansea girls in particular, a giggle of recognition almost before we start to read:

Promenade-Man
'And on Sunday nights, after chapel, he'd be swaggering with his pals along the prom, whistling after the girls.

Girl
Does your mother know you're out? Go away now. Stop following us.   [Another girl titters]

Girl

Don't you say nothing, Hetty, you're only encouraging. No thank you, Mr. Cheeky, with your cut-glass accent and your father's trilby! I don't want no walk on no sands. What d'you say? Ooh listen to him. Het, he's swallowed a dictionary. No, I don't want to go with nobody up no lane in the moonlight, see, and I'm not a baby-snatcher neither. I seen you going to school along Terrace Road, Mr Glad-Eye, with your satchel and wearing your red cap and all. You seen me wearing my . . . no you never. Hetty, mind your glasses! Hetty Harris, you're as bad as them. Oh go away and do your homework, you. No I'm not then. I'm no body's homework, see. Cheek! Hetty Harris don't you let him! Ooh, there's brazen! Well, just to the end of the prom, if you like. No further mind . . . '

Promenade-Man

Oh yes, I knew him well. I've known him by the thousands . . . '

Pulpit Humour of Earlier Days

Many Welsh chapel, and church, goers today maintain that the days of great preaching are over. The time when preachers could keep a congregation enthralled for an hour or more are long gone. But the modern preacher faces considerable competition in proclaiming his 'good news'. The spoken word is no longer the main means of communication. In the fiercely competitive mass-media marketplace, he has to find techniques that will enable him to convey the message of the Bible and also try to convince people to lead Christian lives. Strangely enough, he might do well to return to some of the techniques employed by the Victorian preachers and *Y Barwniaid* (Barons) or *Hoelion Wyth* (Eight Inch Nails) as the earlier Welsh divines were called.

One of their most successful ploys was the use of *pictorial hooks*. These were striking and vivid images sometimes tinged with humour. They were parabolic and enabled the preachers to teach God's loving activity in the lives of men and women, and in particular the historical coming of Jesus Christ. They were modern parables of their day.

C.H. Dodd in his *Parables of the kingdom* conveys fully this pictorial element.

• • •

At its simplest, it is something drawn from nature or common life, arresting its hearers with its vividness and leaving the mind in sufficient doubt about its precise explanation to tease it into more active thought.

. . .

A humorous touch to this everyday picture would make it even more appealing – the early divines even considered such a humour to be a gift from God.

'Put hooks in your sermon!' ordered the Rector to his young curate, 'otherwise it will not hold in their minds.'

'But I often introduce thoughts that are pretty,' protested the young man.

'Pretty indeed,' thundered the Rector. 'Why, a row of tea-caddies in a shop window are very pretty, but they are only empty tea-caddies!'

Bishop Hugh Latimer, the great English preacher who was burnt at the stake in 1555, used this method to great effect. In condemning the greedy priests of his day, when preaching at Paul's Cross, he asked them:

> 'And who is the most diligent prelate in all England that passeth all the rest in the doing of his office? I can tell you, for I know who it is. I know him well. But now I think I see you listening and hearkening that I should name him. There is one that passeth all the others . . . I will tell you who it is. It is the devil! Therefore you unpreaching prelates, learn of the devil to be diligent in your office. If you will not learn of God, for shame, learn of the devil!'

. . .

A Roman Catholic priest in Western Ireland in the early years of the nineteenth century combined his rough, homely and genial eloquence and humour to a good purpose to solve the problem of getting the dues from his parishioners. He decided to preach on *The Day of Judgement* and gave a striking and vivid picture of the terrors that awaited the sinners whom had not paid their dues.

• • •

'Yes, on that great day, me and me Lord will be within the altar rails, and me Lord will ask me, 'Father, did yer people attend Mass regularly? (D'you hear that Biddy Hegarty?).

But I will say, 'Yes me Lord'. And then the Lord will ask, 'And do yer people go to confession regularly?'

And I will say, 'Yes, me Lord!'

But when me Lord asks me, 'And Father, did yer people pay their dues?' Ah, ye blaggards! What shall I say for ye at all, at all?'

It is reported that the purse he carried home that morning was heavy.

• • •

The Revd Charles Haddon Spurgeon, the great Baptist preacher of the nineteenth century, had this gift of humour and knew exactly how far to take it. For example, there is his explanation of how God used ordinary human beings.

'Grace is not spoiled by the hollow wooden spout it runs through. God did once speak by an ass to Balaam, but that did not spoil His words. So he speaks now, not simply by an ass, which He often does, but through something even worse than that!'

• • •

On another occasion he castigated those he regarded as 'Crab-tree Christians':

'These have mixed such a vast amount of vinegar and such tremendous quantity of gall in their constitutions, that they can hardly speak one good word to another. They are like isolated ice-bergs; no one cares to go near them; they float in the sea of forgetfulness until they are at last melted and gone; though good souls, we shall be happy enough to meet them in Heaven; but we shall be precious glad to get rid of them on earth.'

Humour without sound exegesis often results in a literal and an anachronistic form of preaching. It is so easy to misuse the Biblical texts. There are people who will open the pages of the Bible at random, and accept the literal meaning of the first verse that catches their eye as being Divine Guidance. It was a common joke in the Middle Ages to call the laity *asses*. A certain preacher of a later period pointed out that parsons were to work vigorously, while the laity were to attend quietly. To support his contention he quoted Job. 1. 14, 'The oxen were lowing and the asses were feeding beside them'. Another preacher of the post-tobacco period wanted Biblical proof to condemn the habits of smoking and drinking. He found it, or at least misconstrued it, in the words of Isaiah. 'The harp and the lute, the tabret and the pipe and the wine are in their feasts.'

The pictorial hooks technique also has its dangers. The Neapolitan Dominican Monk, Gabriel Berletta, related this coarse and exaggerated Easter Fable.

• • •

When Christ the Lord arose, several persons offered to carry the glad tidings of his Resurrection to his mother. But each one was rejected as unfit for the purpose.

Adam said, 'I should be the one to do it, because I was the cause of evil'. But the Lord answered him,

'Thou likest figs and mightest tarry on the way'.

Abel desired to go, but the Lord said to him,

'On no account; thou mightest meet Cain, who might slay thee.'

Then Noah proposed to deliver the message, but the Lord said to him, 'Thou must not go because thou lovest drink.' The penitent thief would fain have set out on the journey, but he could not because his legs were broken. There was nothing for it but to send an angel, who saluted the Queen of Heaven with a *Hallelujah*.

• • •

Such an extravagant and anachronistic treatment of a sacred subject can only confuse. It is a sad state of affairs for the church when learning is divorced from belief. Bishop South's reply to the claim that God has no need of our learning was, 'God has less need of our ignorance'. Humour demands a naturalness that is not always found in the preacher when he ascends into the pulpit. Whitfield, because of this humour, could make his congregation laugh or cry by merely proclaiming 'Mesopotamia'.

The Humour of 'The Eight-inch nails'

Many older generation Welsh chapel goers are convinced that the great days of preaching ended with the death of the Revd Philip Jones of Porth-cawl (1855-1945). According to them, this was the last *Preaching Baron*, or *Hoelen Wyth* (Eight-Inch Nail), as they were known.

When Dame Sybil Thorndyke was performing in *Macbeth* in the same area of Glamorgan as Philip was preaching, the attendance at *Macbeth* was reported to be 'thin'. There is little doubt that the stage lost some of its finest actors because the 'Barons' had been called to the Christian Ministry. They were masters of dramatic art and could manipulate any congregation to the degree of having them crying one moment, and laughing their heads off the next.

Philip Jones in particular was an expert on alliteration and the short pithy sentence. He described his age as one 'of paint, powder and players of wine, women and woodbine'. The ten maidens of the parable in Matthew 25, 1-13 were described as: 'And five of them were wise and five of them were otherwise'. He claimed to preach in the language of the kitchen and the workroom. *Classic Glamorgan* he called it. He often took his texts from some of the most unfamiliar sections of *The Bible*, such as the *Book of Numbers and Esther*. Some objected to his ability to mock, but he managed to get away with this most dangerous ploy with the humour that he injected into it. Here is an example:

These people are certainly not the cream of our country. My friends, they are merely the ice-creamers!

He had the ability to paint word-pictures and analogies that conveyed more in a sentence than many managed in a whole sermon. On his election to the chair of the Welsh Methodist Assembly, he succeeded a chairman who was six feet tall. Philip was small of stature, and looked even smaller standing next to his predecessor. When he accepted *The Bible* as a confirmation of his office, Philip related the story of the farmer whose chickens had not laid any eggs. In order to persuade the chickens to do their work the farmer bought a large ostrich egg, placed it among the chickens and wrote on it: *Look at this and do your best.*

Another time, he had been preaching with another minister at a special service in a remote village in North Wales. At the end of the service they were dismayed to find that no transport had been arranged to take them to the station. Philip decided to walk there while his friend waited for a lift. Philip was half way to the station when his friend passed in the back of a pop lorry and waved, shouting mockingly, 'Ha, ha, at last I have the better of you'. 'Well, well', muttered Philip. 'That's the biggest pop bottle I have ever seen.'

On another occasion, Philip was trying to drive home how important it was to be humble, and he recited the story of the man in the USA who had ridden a white horse around the countryside warning the people of the oncoming floods, and had saved hundreds of lives. This man went to heaven and was warmly greeted by Peter. The man was very proud of what he had done, and took every opportunity to remind everyone in heaven of his foresight and bravery. He was, however, very disturbed and upset because every time he started to relate his exploit, an old white bearded man got up and went out. The American complained to Peter, saying that he thought the old man very ignorant to do that.

'Don't worry about him', was Peter's advice. 'His name is Noah.'

Even on his deathbed his humour did not wane. 'And how are you, old friend?' his closest friend asked him. 'It's like this', was the faint reply. 'When our local station master found that the train had arrived and had to blow his whistle for it to depart, he found that the dry pea had fallen out of his whistle and was lost. He ran to the local fruiterer, but could only get a split pea. When he blew his whistle, only half the train went out. Half of my train has gone. I'm waiting for the final whistle.'

There were all kinds of stories, and even legends, woven around such great personalities. A Revd J.C. Jones of north Wales was not only a notable preacher, but also a budding politician as well. He was an ardent member of the Labour Party and found it impossible to believe that anyone could vote for any other party. He took every opportunity, both from the pulpit and the political platform, to persuade people to vote his way. One area he visited had swung towards the Liberals and he was determined to convince them of the error of their ways. He told them about the farm labourer who was so fed up with his nasty master that he threw a rope over a beam in the cowshed and hung himself. His master, searching for him the following morning, found him hanging there. 'Well Ifor bach,' said the master. 'What will you do next?'

He was called to settle a dispute that had arisen between two factions in a local church. He related to them the following tale, and then left them to their own devices.

Two friends went to the seashore to bathe. One immediately took off his clothes and dived into the sea. The other stayed on the shore. In a little while he heard his friend shouting, 'Help, save me!' He dashed into the sea and grabbed his friend by the hair, but his hair came off. 'Help, save me!' yelled his friend going down for the second time. He grabbed his arm, but his arm came off. Still the man shouted to be saved. 'Yes, I will save you,' he said, 'if only you will stay together.'

• • •

One of the last such preachers was the late Joseph James (1878-1963) of Llandysilio in Dyfed. He was a very able scholar and his slight stutter helped to enhance his style and delivery. He was described as 'fifteen stones of humour' and this enchanting aspect of his personality enabled him to remain for many years in the two churches of Llandysilio and Llawhaden.

He was the proud owner of a Trojan car and it was an event in the village when Joe ventured forth in this vehicle. On one occasion he had to visit the doctor because of the arthritis in his right arm. The doctor asked him what kind of car he was running and immediately realised that the trouble was due to the starting handle of the Trojan. 'What you have, Mr James, is not arthritis but Trojanitis,' the doctor told him.

Joe was seen driving the wrong way up a one way street in the city of Swansea. This caused a passer-by some consternation, and he shouted; 'Hey you, this is one way'.

'Well, that's alright then,' was the reply. 'It's only one way I want to go.'

He was a well-known and popular lecturer on such topics as 'the New Theology', 'Communism', and 'Tutankhamen'. His opening remark on the latter was, 'Now, I wonder what his mother called him'.

In his lecture on 'the New Theology', he referred to its relationship to 'the Old Theology', and the way some folk deceived themselves into thinking that the old one was still alive. To drive home his point, he related the story of the Irish servant who was ordered by his master to kill the cockerel. The servant beheaded the bird, but it kept running around without its head.

'Didn't you kill that cockerel, Paddy?' enquired the master.

'Oh yes I did sir, I've killed it all right. He's dead enough sir, but he doesn't know it yet!'

Joe was a good pastor and made it his duty to visit all of his members. One bright sunny morning he made his way to one of the local farms. The farmer had always striven to give the impression that he was a pious and righteous man. At the Tuesday prayer meeting, he was constantly on his knees giving a prolonged prayer and telling the Almighty all the local news. As Joe approached the entrance to the farm he could hear loud hammering, followed by a string of invectives hardly suitable for the prayer meeting. The farmer was nursing a bleeding finger when Joe appeared but, as soon as he caught sight of Joe, he started to hum a hymn tune. The sheepdogs accompanying the farmer came forward to greet Joe with their tails wagging and the farmer greeted him in the most sober fashion. They chatted for a while and when the time came for Joe to leave, he turned to the farmer and said; 'Now William, don't forget to change the names of those dogs, there's a good fellow'.

The late Professor Evans of Memorial College, Brecon (who was one hundred when he introduced the Queen on one of her Christmas Broadcasts), used to recall the sermons and the incidents in the lives of the great preaching barons that he had heard as a man and boy. He always maintained that the barons could only preach effectively in the Welsh language. The language lent itself to this particular kind of communication because it so onomatopoeic, more so than English. He used to compare such words as 'peace' with the Welsh equivalent *Tangnefedd*, or 'pot' with its equivalent *crochan*. The Welsh words could be sustained and move one into the *Hwyl*, whereas their English equivalents had hardly expressed their meaning at all.

He remembered how the Revd Philip Jones had made his dramatic entry in one of the local Methodist chapels on one occasion, emerging suddenly from the vestry to face a packed congregation and causing a hush to descend upon the packed gathering. Philips paused several times as he made his way to the pulpit, and every time he stopped, he glanced over his shoulder, uttering a little cry.

This continued while he was preaching and the congregation by the end of the sermon had become intrigued by the performance. Then, as he gave his peroration, he suddenly stopped, looked over his shoulder, and cried out 'Williams Pantycelyn! So, you are here after all!' and then broke out into the *Hwyl* as he recited one of Williams's most famous hymns:

'Yn Eden cofiaf hynny byth,
Bendithion gollais rif y gwlith.'

(From Eden, will I ever forget,
Blessings I lost as numerous as the dew.)

He declared at the end of his hour-long sermon that
Williams had managed to put into one verse all that he,
Philips, had been trying to say all evening.

The Humour of the Revd Stephen Jenkins

Stephen Jenkins was born in 1815 and was known to be strong in mind and body. His very presence gave the impression of endurance and strength. Cynddylan Jones, one of the *Barons* proclaimed:

> God is a lover of the useful, my friends. When He framed the crust of the earth He could have made it of silver and gold and precious stones, but instead he made it of coal and lime and iron and granite. Not so beautiful, my friends, but far more useful.

This was the way people thought of Stephen Jenkins – he was certainly not beautiful, but he was very useful. Educated at the Old Calvinistic Chapel in Llechryd, where his cousin the notable Enoch Stephens was headmaster, he was a regular attender of Sunday School and became a teacher and examiner of the catechism. From the age of twelve he worked at the local quarry, and even at this tender age he showed a real sense of humour that made him popular among his fellow workers.

He also displayed a mischievous streak. He once discovered that there was a secret distillery in the village. One night he dressed up as a customs officer and marched up to the door of the secret hideout, demanding entry as a revenue officer. He struck terror into those involved in the malt distilling process and, before running away through a back entrance, they poured the precious liquid into the nearby stream. When they eventually returned, they found Stephen having a good old laugh. The chapel people praised him for ridding the village of the clandestine activity, but he would not have been so popular with the rest of the village.

When he became the manager of the quarry, he married a young widow and moved to another village where they settled down happily and eventually had four daughters. They became members of the local Calvinistic Methodist Church and played a leading role in the chapel activities. Stephen claimed that he had been 'converted' but not in the sweeping 'revolutionary' manner. He described it as a gradual 'evolutionary' conversion, just like the acorn growing into an oak tree.

He was a passionate coracle fisherman, but the experience of losing a friend in a coracling accident was to change the course of his life. He was teaching his friend the art of coracling when the flimsy vessel overturned, drowning the friend. Shortly after this distressing incident, Stephen decided to enter the Christian ministry. With little or no training, he was 'called' to the English church in the village of Crundale, near Hwlffordd (Haverfordwest) where he developed a unique style of preaching. His message was simple and his language was that of the farming community. He was genial and blunt, but never rude; he used humorous, droll and anachronistic illustrations that had home truths embedded in them. Due to his lack of academic knowledge, he found that his appeal as a popular preacher was in clothing the most ancient images in modern phraseology, and he seemed completely unaware of the humour involved.

He used to refer to the 'Mayor of Mesopotamia', the 'Marquis of Galilee' and the 'Squire of Padanaran'. The guards at Jesus' tomb he called 'Sowldyers in their red coats'. This is how he described Belshazzar's Feast:

'The king and all the princes and the lords, the dukes and the earls and baronets were assembled in the biggest room in the Royal Palace, and there were fine goings on there. But by and by, there came a sudden stop and they all turns pale as death.

'What is wrong with you people? Why don't you go on with your wine and comic songs, your dancing and your revels?'

Ah no, they couldn't, for right there before them was The Hand, a-writing upon the wall, over the candlestick, and they couldn't help a-seeing it. And the king was a-shaking and a-trembling from head to foot; and he says,

'Call in the old professors of the University. Call them clever conjurors and soothsayers. Bring in them able magicians.'

And they comes in, but not one of them could read nor make any meaning of the writing on the wall. And the king was a-shivering and a-shaking with fear.

Just then the queen comes in and she said to him; 'Don't be afraid, Belshazzar, honey. I know one man in the city that will be able to read and explain the meaning of the writing on the wall. Don't you mind that Daniel the Jew, that used to tell thy old father's dreams after everyone else had failed?'

So Daniel was called.

'If you please, madam,' said Daniel to the queen at the door; 'I would rather not go in for I have never been to a ball in my life!'

'Never mind, Daniel bach,' said the queen. 'All their

merriment is over now and you can venture to go in. They are sober enough now.' So Daniel went in.

'Can you make out that writing on the wall?' asked the trembling king.

'Can I?' answered Daniel. 'Ay, for certain I can! It is as plain as ABC to me. It is only a line of my heavenly Father's shorthand writing.'

That night, Belshazzar, the king of the Chaldeans was slain. My dear people, take care that you don't sin against God. For you don't know how, or when, his awful judgement will come upon you!'

The band played as before
While reading the third chapter of *The Book of Daniel*, Stephen found a novel way of getting over a linguistic difficulty. In one chapter the same verse appears four times listing musical instruments. The first time he read the verse he managed to pull through, only with some difficulty.

That at what time ye hear the sound of the cornet, flute, harp, sacbut, psaltery, dulcimer and all kinds of music.

The second and third time that he came to the verse, he didn't do so well, and found the pronunciations awkward. On the fourth reading he found the answer, and read out with the utmost seriousness; 'And the band played on'.

Prejudice
He described 'prejudice' as 'trying to put water into a bottle with the cork in it. Take the cork out with the corkscrew of brotherly love, and you can fill the bottle easy enough'.

The Tin Can

At the monthly meeting in Haverfordwest, things were dragging along and the speakers could not get any *hwyl* into the proceedings. The chairman called on Stephen to say a few words.

'I remember some time ago my friends,' he said, 'that a preacher came to Crundale on the Saturday afternoon, a little earlier than expected. The farmer and his wife, where he was to stay, were very busy. The mistress went to put the kettle on, but the tin can was empty.

'Here Mary,' she said to the maid. 'Run to the well as fast as you can.'

When the mistress went to put water in the kettle on the maid's return, there wasn't a drop in the can. What was the matter? Was the well dry? No! There was plenty of water in the well. Was the tin can leaking? No! What was the matter then? SHE PUT THE TIN CAN IN THE WELL WITHOUT TAKING THE LID OFF! It seems to me, friends, that we in this meeting are as dull as Mary. We've come to the Well of Salvation with our tin cans without taking the lids off!

The farmers wife and her apron

To illustrate the verse, 'Thou openest thine hand, they are filled with good,' (Psalm CIV, v28) Stephen gave the following parable.

'I dare say you've noticed the farmer's wife coming out of the house in the morning, with a big apron full of corn for the fowls. She don't need to call them, they know her step and the sounds of her clogs. They knows the old apron a long way off, and they comes to her from every place. The old gander leads the geese and all the little goslings to her; and the old hens takes their chicks to her, and the turkeys hurry to her with their young uns. Then she puts her hands into the old apron and throws a handful here and there, this way and that way, till they are all satisfied. So our Heavenly Father throws his great blessings this way to the north, that way to the south, this way to the east and that way to the west.

The widow of Nain's son

His sermon on the 'resurrection of the son of the widow of Nain' went as follows:-

'A poor widow from a little town in Galilee had lost her only son. She went to the gravedigger to ask him to get a grave ready for him. And the gravedigger was very glad of the job. On the day of the funeral the gravedigger was watching for the funeral to come, for him to go and ring the bell to call the parson to meet the coffin at the gate, and to read the burial service. But there was no sign of the funeral coming and the gravedigger was getting anxious and was asking everyone; 'Did you see a funeral on the way?'

'No,' they said.

'Well, well', he said, 'it is over an hour late now'. Then he asked another man.

'No, for certain', that one said again.

'Dear me', said the gravedigger. 'It is over two hours late.'

At last, he thought he saw the funeral coming up the hill to the church so he went to ring the bell to call the parson, who came in his white gown and his prayer book in his hand and began to read the burial service.

'I am the Resurrection and the life', he said.

'No, no', said one of the people that had brought back the empty coffin. You aren't the Resurrection and the life. It was Him that met the funeral on the way, and stopped it. He made us put the coffin down and open the lid of the coffin, and He took the dead man by the hand and said to him, 'Young man, I say to thee, arise.' And sure enough, he got up alive out of the coffin, and has gone home with his poor widow mother.'

The gravedigger sat listening to every word and he asked the people. 'Is it true?'

'Ay for certain 'tis true; we saw it with our own eyes.'

'Well, well,' said the gravedigger. 'If that is the case, then my occupation is clean gone! Him or me in the same place is enough, and I don't know who is going to pay me. And I don't know whether He has been paid yet.'

That old bird

When Peter went to Caeserea to his preaching appointment, he took Mrs Peter with him. The farmer took Peter around the farm to show him the stock. On the way the bull roared at him, but he didn't take any notice. When he came to the farmyard the gander came hissing after him, and he didn't mind that either. But all of a sudden the old cock came up to him quite bold and sang cock-a doodle-do, and he turned quite pale. When he went into the house, Mrs Peter asked, 'What's the matter Peter bach?'

'Oh, that old bird again', he said.

And there he was awaking in the night, and asking Mrs Peter.

'D'you hear that old bird again?'

Ah my dear people. If you forget your Saviour, or deny

him, old conscience will remind you of it in some way or another, even after you've been forgiven!

The little maid
Another time when he was on the theme of Peter's denial, he said

'What surprises me is that Peter should deny his Master for fear of a little maid. If it had been some grand lady with a big chain on her neck, and gold rings on her fingers, and a grand silk dress a-rustling about the place, it would have been something. But to deny Him for fear of a little servant maid that was putting balls (culm) on Pilate's fire, that does surprise me.'

Jonah
Stephen waxed eloquent over Jonah's adventures.

'Jonah was a noted preacher in many ways. And the thing he was specially noted for was that he was the only preacher that ever went to a certain place, and came out alive. Namely, the whale's belly! The whale's belly was Jonah's college.

He learned more in there than students of the local college learn in three years. Jonah was the inside passenger, because the Lord did not want to make a jockey of him.'

Noah
These are sections from Stephen's famous sermon on *Noah's Ark*.

'An Ark?' says Noah, 'What's an Ark?'
'A great big ship,' says the Lord.
'But I don't know what a ship is,' says Noah.

'It is like a big house that can swim on water, and is made out of wood.'

'But I don't know what you mean.' It was no use God trying to tell old Noah what it was. So God gave him a plan and a picture of the Ark, and told him to make it exactly like the plan and the picture.

'And mind whatever you do, make it watertight as I am going to bring down heavy rain from the sky!'

'Rain?' said Noah, 'what is rain? I don't know what rain is!' And how was he to know, for the ground was watered by dew until then . . . But the people won't believe him and come there week after week, month after month, mocking old Noah and telling him he was a big fool to waste his time.

And they was daily asking him, 'Noah, where is the rain?'

'I don't know,' he kept saying. 'But it is sure to come, for God told me and God can't tell a lie.'

'Here Shem,' said he. 'You take the measuring rod in your hand and measure the biggest elephant you can see, and we'll make a door big enough for him to get in.' But when they was a-going to put the door on its hinges, young Japheth came running, almost out of breath, and said to old Noah,

'Do you know father, as I was climbing the hill over there, I saw a great big animal, taller by far than the biggest elephant. For certain he'll never get in by that door.'

'Well,' said Noah, 'he will have to bend to get in, for there is no time to make a new door.' . . . And there was Mrs Noah, looking through the window, and she saw the Mayor of Mesopotamia driving at full speed to the Ark.

She says to old Noah,

'Open the door Noah bach; here's the Mayor of Mesopotamia coming.'

'No matter who is coming, God has closed the door! It is too late,' said Noah. Then she looked again and saw a royal carriage driving through the water with the king and queen in it.

'Open the door Noah. Here come the king and queen.'

'No matter who is there, Mrs Noah, God has closed the door. It is too late.' Then Mrs Noah looked again through the window and saw a poor mother struggling up to her neck in water, holding her dear baby as high as ever she could out of the rising flood, and Mrs Noah says to Noah:

'Oh Noah, honey, do open the door for pity's sake. Here is a poor mother with her baby almost drowning, and struggling to get in.'

'Too late, too late,' Noah cried. 'God has closed the door and no man can open it. I have preached repentance to that woman ever since she was a baby herself. But she only laughed at me, and now it is too late!'

How much for your thoughts

Stephen Jenkins was not slow at repartee. One Sunday after dinner, a young deacon from the Independent Chapel where Stephen was preaching that day found Stephen meditating over his evening sermon.

'How much for your thoughts Mr Jenkins?' the young man asked.

'Well,' was the reply. 'Your father used to give me only fifteen shillings; I don't know whether you are going to improve on that?'

The artist and the beggar

Jenkins was able to transform a well-known anecdote and make it sound strange, even to its original author.

'An able painter, living in the West End of London, told his servant one day that if he should ever meet a character like the Prodigal Son, he was to do his best to get him to his master's house. He was to tell him that he would get a handsome reward. Nothing will make people do anything, my friends, like a reward.

His servant found a beggar and persuaded him to go with him to his master. The artist was delighted to see the beggar, and told him, 'Come as you are now, I prays you; bare headed, bare backed, bare legged . . . don't alter yourself one bit, and I will give you a handsome reward.'

Next morning the old beggar came. He had washed his face and combed his hair and had someone else's boots on. He had patched himself up for the occasion.

When the artist saw him, he said, 'You've disobeyed my orders. Go away! You be no good to me now. If only you'd come as you was, I would have given you a good reward. But now, go away!' And that is how it is with us. You need to come to the saviour as you are.

Jenkins and the devil

Jenkins had no doubts about the reality and personality of the devil. Speaking at a Temperance meeting in Haverfordwest, he said:

'I remember, forty years ago, old Satan could be seen marching up and down the houses with his top coat on, and saying about the people and the houses; 'All these belong to me.' But last week he could be seen slinking away up that hill . . . like a beaten dog.'

Feeding the devil

In the Gospel Tent in Cardiff he told the congregation:

'You people in Cardiff here do complain that old Satan is too strong for you. But what wonder is it that he is too strong for you when you fed him so well? You went out of the house this morning without a word of family prayer. That was a good breakfast to begin with. Then you come home to your dinner in an evil passion, and that was another hearty meal for him. And you're feeding him like that all day and every day. What wonder is it that he is too strong for you when you're feeding him so much? Take my advice, my dear people, and starve the old devil out.'

Stephen Jenkins on 'Daniel in the Lions' Den'

The officers of King Darius were very jealous of the fame and position of Daniel, but couldn't find fault in him so as to complain to the king, apart from his religion. So they decided that they would persuade the proud king to make a decree that no one should pray to God or man; only to him. If anyone would dare disobey the law, he should be cast into the lions' den. And the king passed the law and signed the decree, for he had no idea that it was done on purpose against Daniel.

The jealous officers went away to watch Daniel's house, to see if he would keep the law. When the hour of prayer was come, they saw Daniel opening the window facing the Holy City. They came under his window like a lot of spies to hearken, and there was Daniel a-praying to the God of his fathers. And they say to one another,

'Now we've caught him fine. He won't lord it over us any more.' And away they goes to the king and says, 'Do you know that there Daniel the Jew, your Majesty? Well, he don't care a bit about you, or your laws. There he is a-praying to his God, after your Majesty passed a law that nobody was to pray, only to you.' And the king was very angry, but sorry that it was Daniel that was the first to have to face the den of lions.

'Will you please sign the warrant?' they say to the king. He wasn't willing to sign it for a long time, but they made him sign it by telling him to remember that it was the law of the Medes and Persians, that altereth not. So the king, unwillingly, signed the warrant with his hand a-trembling all the time. They took the warrant and showed it to Daniel and said to him, 'You are our prisoner, and you must come with us to be tried for breaking the law, by praying'.

And there was a great trial and Daniel was condemned to be cast into the lions' den. And as he was going down the High Street, all the little orphans of the city were following him and a-crying and saying, 'What shall we do now? They are taking our best friend to the lions' den!' And all the poor widows of the city were weeping, 'Oh Daniel, oh Daniel! What shall we do? What will become of us?' And there were Shadrach, Meshech and Abednego holding a prayer meeting to ask the Lord to save Daniel from the lions' den like he had saved them from the fiery burning furnace.

After putting a royal seal on the door of the den, the king goes home to the royal palace very low in spirits. By and by his butler comes in to the king and asks, 'What will your Majesty please to have for your supper tonight?'

'No supper tonight,' says the king. 'Daniel is in the lions' den!' Then the leader of the band comes in and asks, 'Please your Majesty, what music shall we play tonight?'

'No music tonight,' says the king. 'Daniel is in the lions' den!' Then the chambermaid comes in and brings in the candles saying, 'Please your Majesty, your bed is ready.'

'No bed tonight,' says he. 'Daniel is in the lions' den!' There was no sleep that night and he was getting up very often to see if there was sign of daybreak. And so glad he was to see the morning dawn after such a night.

My friends, there is a morning dawn after the longest night in the world, but if you goes to the place of torment, that will be eternal night without the morning dawn!

As soon as the king was dressed he ran down all the way in his slippers to the lions' den and looked through the bars. There was Daniel lying down, a-sleeping quite comfortable. That was one lion under his feet like a grand cushion and another under him like a seat and another under his head like a pillow. He had a far more comfortable night than the king and his princes.

And the king put his mouth to the bars of the den and shouted, 'D-d-d-d-dan, are you living?'

And Daniel answered, 'O king, live for ever for my God has sent his angel to shut the mouths of the lion, and I am all right'. The officers in charge opened the doors of the den and let Daniel out, and the king took him, arm-in-arm, to the Royal Palace and there was great joy in the city. The king sent the guards to take Daniel's enemy and put them in prison, and that was a fine breakfast for them hungry lions. Put your faith in Daniel's God and he will save you from the devil and his angels, who go about like roaring lions seeking whom they may devour.

Jenkin's remedy for a late riser

'I had a servant-maid one time that wouldn't get up of a-morning when I called her. I had to call her a dozen times before she would rise. However, she was a good maid, only to try to get her up.

She came to me one night and asked me to call her early the next morning, so that she could do her work before going to Pembroke fair.

'But you don't get up when I call you, maid!' I said.

'Do call me master, tomorrow morning early, and I will get up,' she said.

At six o'clock in the morning, I called her and she answered as usual. I was determined not to call her the second time. As I was passing her room to go downstairs, I knew by her heavy snoring that she was a-sleeping fast again. I lit the fire and made my own breakfast, and went to the shop till dinnertime. But the maid has not come down, so I got my own dinner and went to the shop again till teatime. At half-past four I went to get my tea and, as I was coming in the house, the maid was a-coming down the stairs.

'You are coming back early from the fair, maid, aren't you? It's only half-past four.'

I wasn't looking to scold her, but it was a certain cure for her late rising. I had no trouble to get her up of a-morning after that.

• • •

Stephen Jenkins showed in his preaching that rare ability of inventiveness that enabled him to create modern parables that were full of humour. Unfortunately, his lack of education condemned him to an anachronistic style that has been rediculed by those blessed with a greater degree of learning.

The Humour of John Jones

John Jones of Caerfyrddin (Carmarthen) possessed that genial, homely and bluntly unconscious humour that is found in certain Welsh characters. He was small of stature with a round face and twinkling eyes that winked when he was about to launch into a humorous account. Many considered him devoid of ordinary common sense, but others acknowledge that he was exceptionally wise and witty, and certainly no ordinary human being! He was generous and playful by nature, and a most lovable person who hated hypocrisy and treated everyone as equals.

He lived at the end of the nineteenth century in a thatched cottage that had earthen walls and floor, with just two downstairs rooms. There was a small garden with an orchard, through which ran a lively brook. He had managed to get some extra land nearby where he kept four cows, a donkey and a horse. Since there wasn't enough work for him on his own land he helped on the neighbouring farms, and anywhere else, where he could boost his meagre income. Many of the local farmers gave him work just to have his entertaining company. At the end of the working day, the farmer and his family gathered in the large kitchen for their evening meal. John would be a welcome guest, and they would all eagerly wait for the winking, pipe smoking John to entertain them. He never disappointed.

He was very fond of his pint of ale, and no one attempted to preach temperance to him. He had a wife and three children but it was claimed that he might have had more children. Peggy his wife, a woman with a wild and unruly temperment, caused no end of trouble and worry to the carefree John. She died some years before him and John lived to a ripe old age.

John's way of keeping a pig
He had an unique way of keeping his pigs, which involved feeding them one day and starving them the next. When a neighbour asked why he did this, he was told:

'I am very fond of striped bacon see, and this is the only way to get it!'

The clogs
'How are you today, John?' a neighbour enquired.

'Not very good man,' was the reply. 'It's Dafi the cobbler's clogs that is the trouble. I cannot walk in them. They were saying in Sunday School about binding the devil's feet. If he had this pair of Dafi's clogs, he wouldn't go very far I can tell you.'

John goes courting
Peggy, his wife, was in service at the local *plas* (mansion), and John would visit her twice a week by night. He tried to be quiet and discrete about his visits but one night, the squire found John standing outside, flashing a lantern at the kitchen window.

'And what in heaven's name might you be doing here at this time of night, may I ask?' demanded the squire.

'Courting sir,' was the reply.

'You're lying John Jones!' the squire said angrily. 'And what are you doing with that lantern for goodness sake? I never used one when I did my courting.'

'No sir, that is obvious,' came the sudden riposte.

John and the parson

John and the local parson were bosom pals, John attending his church occasionally although he was 'chapel'. He was of the opinion that it didn't really matter where one worshipped because we would all end up in the same place.

John was ploughing the parson's field. At mid-day the parson came to look for him and found John sitting in the hedge with the horses grazing quietly nearby.

'Now look here John, this is not good enough,' chided the parson. 'You should take the opportunity to trim that hedge while the horses are grazing!'

'And I will do just that when you take an apron with you into that pulpit and peel a few potatoes while the congregation is singing the hymns!'

John and his wife

One day while enjoying a smoke, his children started to tease him. One of the girls asked him where 'paradise' was.

'There are two answers to that question,' was the reply. 'Firstly, I can tell you that it is not very far away from us. It's just a day's journey away because Jesus said to the thief on the cross – today, thou shalt be with me in paradise. Secondly, when your mother goes off to visit your grandfather and decides to stay over for a few days, then it's paradise here.'

Unchained melody

John was feeding a farmer's draught horses following a heavy day in the fields. The brace of geldings and brace of mares, all of them bay Shires, were shining beautifully having been carefully groomed, and were dreamily munching their oats to the accompaniment of John imitating an unimaginative blackbird. The Methodist preacher was on an errand to the farm and entered the stable to discover the reason for the whistling. The whistler informed him that the sound of the whistle helped the great horses pass water following a heavy days work. The intrigued minister informed John that he himself had some trouble with the water works and John suggested that the minister occupy the empty stall at the end, just to see if the whistling might help.

A minute later, the minister informed John that he was ready, and the whistling resumed. Some time passed, with the sound of munching oats being rather spoiled by some groans coming from the far stall. However, the minister at last spoke, saying rather hurriedly;

'I think, John Jones, that you might be whistling the wrong tune.'

The lecture
John had been round to a neighbour entertaining as usual and was very late going home. A lecture had been given at the local chapel and a neighbour saw John hurrying home.

'Been to the lecture?' the neighbour enquired.

'No, no,' was the hurried reply. 'Going to one!'

John and the preacher
A particularly boring lay preacher was taking the chapel service, and arrived soaked to the skin.

'I'm drenched,' protested the unfortunate man. 'What shall I do?'

'You go to the pulpit, friend,' instructed John. 'You'll be dry enough there.'

John the sleeper

John was well known for sleeping during the sermon, but he would never admit it.

'You slept today again,' Peggy said accusingly.

'How d'you know that?'

'You had your eyes closed all the time,' she said.

'Now that's where you are wrong woman. I listen better with my eyes closed you see.'

'But you were nodding as well,' persisted Peggy.

'There you are then! It just shows how much I agree with the preacher. In any case, how could anyone sleep with that preacher making so much of a fuss in that pulpit?'

John and sorrow

A close friend died and John felt the loss greatly.

'Don't worry about him,' his other friend said, trying to comfort him. 'He's gone to a better place, and by now he'll be playing the harp with the angels.'

'Duw!' exclaimed John. 'He's quickly become very clever, because when he was down here he couldn't even play the penny whistle.'

When another friend died John went to pay his last respects. He found his friend lying in a coffin with his violin laid next to him.

'You've put his violin in with him,' said John to the widow.

'Yes, I have,' she said. 'He was such a good fiddle player, and he loved his old violin.'

'Lucky he didn't play the piano!' said John.

John and the stolen horse

A gypsy stole John's horse and was subsequently brought before the local magistrates. The gypsy maintained that the horse was his, and had been for some years. John was present but had not produced any witnesses. The magistrates were about to release the gypsy and give him the benefit of the doubt. At this point, John appealed to the magistrates, claiming that he could prove that it was his horse. The magistrates agreed to let John do so. John threw a sack over the horse's head and asked the gypsy to point to the horse's blind eye. After a pause the gypsy pointed to the right eye.

John pulled the sack off the animal's head and declared that the horse could see with both eyes. The magistrates gave their verdict in John's favour.

Push you pull me

John went to the saddler to buy one spur. The saddler pointed out that spurs were sold in pairs.

'That's ridiculous!' protested John. 'If I get one side of the horse to go, the other has to follow.'

The legacy

A neighbour was surprised that he had been left so much money in the will of a person who had seen him only once in his life.

'It would be more of a surprise if he had seen you more than once,' was John's comment.

John and booze

John was weaving and swaying his way home from the local fair after a heavy drinking session.

'Drunk again John!' said the parson.

'Yes, and me as well,' was the drunken reply.

John and the borrower

A particular neighbour was a nuisance, constantly wanting to borrow something or another. One morning he asked John if he could borrow the donkey to carry some goods to Caerfyrddin market.

"Sorry mawr and all that,' said John, 'but I've already lent it to Tomos Pen-yr-allt.' At that moment the donkey, which was still in the stable, began to bray.

'See!' said the neighbour. 'He's saying that you are a first class liar John Jones.'

'Well I'll be damned,' John retorted. 'You mean you'd rather believe a donkey than a human being.'

The donkey and the pancakes

John's wife was not a particularly good cook. She decided however to give John a surprise and, having plenty of eggs, cooked him some pancakes to welcome him home. As John approached the cottage he heard terrible wailing from within.

'What happened here?' he asked.

'I baked a few pancakes for you and placed them on the doorstep to cool, but that donkey of yours ate the lot.'

'Don't worry yourself about it,' John replied, 'I know where to find another donkey.'

The cobbler's house

The cobbler's house was the village meeting place for the men. John was a regular visitor and often the centre of attention. Twm Coesa Cam (bandy-legs) was sitting close to the fire.

'Terrible wet night, isn't it?' Twm said.

'It must be very wet,' John said, 'because it's warped your legs, that's for sure.'

Another time one of the men asked, 'Has a man with one eye called Lewis called here today?'

'Don't know,' John replied. 'What's the other eye called?'

On another occasion an argument arose between John and one of the men who was carrying a stick.

'There is a great rogue at the end of this stick!' declared the man pointing at John's chest.

'Which end are you talking about?' was the reply.

Later on John complained of a sound in his head.

'The reason is that your head is completely empty!' remarked one companion.

'Don't you get sounds at all in your head then?' asked John.

'No, never,' was the reply.

'A sure sign that your head has a crack in it,' was the instant diagnosis.

The grave digger

John would take on any job to earn a bit extra. He was busy opening a grave when a stranger came over to him.

'Tell me!' the stranger said, 'how often do people die in this area?'

'Only once,' John said, and the stranger walked away a wiser man.

While opening another grave, his friend William came and sat watching him.

'Why do you think that more men die suddenly than women?' his friend asked.

'Oh, I think the women want the last word, as usual!' he was told.

The dirty shirt
His shirt was not as clean as he wanted it to be and he was blaming his wife.

'How long do you wear your shirts then John?' one of his friends asked.

'Just below the knee,' was the unexpected answer.

The rains come
John's relationship with his wife had been a rocky affair. She died before him and was buried in the local cemetery. A dreadful drought followed the event and on the day the weather broke, John met a local farmer who was all smiles.

'Rain at last, John,' the farmer said. 'Everything will now emerge from mother earth for us . . . '

'Duw, I hope not,' was the reply. 'I hope she keeps the wife with her.'

Welsh Miners Humour, When There Were Some Reasons to be Humorous

The mining industry has always been considered a dangerous occupation, but its disappearance from the Welsh Valleys has not brought relief and comfort. The destruction of the industry is nearly complete and, although it endangered the health and the very existence of the miners, there is a deep sadness that, having fought so long and so hard, it is no more.

Coal mining meant a tough and uncomfortable way of earning a living, but it was characterised by independence of spirit and of sacrifice. There was a sense of belonging to a close knit family and it is this relationship and spirit that endures in the valleys, and gives some hope that there will be some light at the end of the very dark slant.

The following are examples of the kind of humour found among the miners in the heydays of this once all-enveloping industry.

The jeep

They were having a break underground and Twm was relating how an American soldier, who had been travelling for a long time, called at a nearby house for a drink of water. The woman who answered the door invited him inside and offered him a cup of tea.

'Many thanks, mam,' the soldier replied. 'But I can't stay long because I have a Jeep outside.'

'Duw, go and bring her in,' the woman said. 'And she can have a cup of tea as well.'

They all laughed, except Norman who looked shocked.

'Just a minute!' said Norman. 'Let Twm finish his story!'

'I have finished, you nut,' Twm said.

'But did he fetch her in then, or did he take the cuppa out to her? I tell you this, my old woman wouldn't have stayed outside! She'd have been in like a shot!'

Sweethearts

'Did you hear the news this morning?' Bob asked his young helper. 'The Russians are in Warsaw and General Patton is on his way to Berlin to finish it off.'

'I don't believe that,' the youngster replied, 'cause Patton, they say, is lost. They've searched every inch of the land from Nancy to Metz, and no sign of him.'

'Why?' Bob asked, 'Are Nancy and Metz places then?'

'Course they are!' the youngster replied.

'Well, well,' said Bob. 'I thought they were sweethearts, just like St Quentin and Lille!'

Funny potato deal

Now then Harry,' said his friend looking at the unopened sack of potatoes. 'Can I take it that they are all good potatoes?'

'I can assure you that there isn't a naughty potato in that bag!'

No alternative

The local minister was unsympathetic towards the miners who, in his opinion, were out on strike too often. Arthur, a miner, was a keen chapel member. One Monday morning down the mine, he asked Jim what he thought of Sunday night's sermon.

'Not much man!' was the reply. 'Think of him telling us that we are all sinners, and that the wages of sin are death! Is there any wonder that we are continually fighting for a living wage?'

A clear explanation
Harry maintained that he was an expert at translating Welsh into English. He knew that the word *llif* in Welsh meant both 'flood' and 'wood-saw', and that 'manure' in Welsh was *tom*.

At the lamp queue one morning the news came that heavy rains had washed away the manure that had been stored for the village allotment. The Englishman among them had not fully grasped the news so Harry took it upon himself to provide an explanation. Unfortunately, the Englishman was not greatly enlightened by; 'There was a big saw in the brook, and tom has been drowned.'

The canon
It was not unusual to find the miners discussing the future education of their children. Jim asked Arthur if his son would be coming to work underground.

'Not on your life, boy!' was the adamant reply. I'm going to do what the manager has done for his son. He sent him to a theological college, and now he is a canon.'

'Tommy rot!' said Jim. 'That can't be true! Saint Paul himself was only a pistol!'

Kind thoughts
Noah and Wil were about to sit down for a bite to eat when Arthur noticed a big stone overhanging, just above Noah's head.

'Don't sit there, you fool!' Arthur yelled at him. 'Can't you see that thing hanging there?'

'The roof is safe enough!' said Noah as he settled down under it.

'Oh well, if that's the way you deacons teach the flock at Bethany, be it on your own head.'

'You don't need to worry about me, son.' Noah said, 'because I am never alone. There's One greater than all of us looking after me.'

'But I'm thinking of you both, man,' was the reply.

Got a stool?

Simon Jenkins, the overman, was made a deacon at Bethany, but he found the big seat rather uncomfortable. To make things much worse, he was spotted by another of the deacons coming out of the *Royal Oak*, bareheaded and much the worse for wear. He was summoned before the other deacons, accused of being drunk, and ordered to vacate the big seat forthwith.

Simon was a bit of a poet and replied to his excommunication in the following vein.

Noah drank till he was blind,
Abram held a knife,
David left his girl behind,
Lot divorced his wife.
Solomon had wives galore,
Moses killed a chap,
St Peter lied, denied and swore,
But Simon only lost his cap.

A tight corner

'Something tells me that this war is going to finish before

long, because people are praying hard for it to stop, and prayers are always answered. What d'you think, Arthur?'

'I don't know about that, Wil. Just think now: the King has been praying; Tojo has been praying, old Goebbels and his goblins have been praying. So what is the Almighty to do? There can only be one victor, so who is he going to give it to I ask you?'

'Yes, yes. I take the point, Wil! He's in a devil of a hole isn't he?'

The resurrection

The finest nightshift haulier died suddenly, and his friends attended his funeral in large numbers. Owing to some confusion the hearse didn't turn up and the men decided to carry the coffin to the Parish Church.

It was a steep climb to the church and they had to stop several times on the way for 'refreshments'. They eventually managed to get to the church and were met by the vicar who led the way, declaring in a loud voice: 'I am the resurrection and the life!'

'Hold on there, father!' cried the well oiled Twm. 'Resurrection indeed! You must be joking after we've carried him all this way!'

The cuckoo

Jim decided that the time had come for him to leave the mine and take a cleaner job in the English Midlands. He was told by the foreman of the firm to call again the next day. When he arrived the following day, he was told to come back in a week. At the end of the week, he called again. This time the manager told him to come back in the spring.

'Now look here' said an infuriated Jim. 'I am a collier from south Wales, and not a blooming cuckoo!'

A real toff

Jim One Pint, the new barman of the *Pony and Trap*, was dressed up to concert pitch by the landlady, with an old collar and top coat that had been discarded by her husband some thirty years before. When the customers first saw him they were greatly amused because Jim had never worn a collar in his life.

'Jim, what's happened to you?' his friend asked. 'You look a real toff today.'

'Yes, well, it is a good show isn't it?' was the reply. 'But remember, it's only a show . . . like a mahogany door on a coal cwtsh!'

Delayed effect

Twm and Dai were visiting London, and found their way to the Joo-joo Club. Whilst there, they were persuaded to try a whiff of opium. It didn't have the expected effect.

'I don't think much of it,' Dai said. 'I'd prefer to smoke Franklin.'

'Hold on now,' said Twm. 'Try another whiff before we go.' The effect was again disappointing. Dai put his cap on and said,

'I'm going.'

'Where to?' asked Twm.

'Home!' Dai said. 'I've got to get to Bridgend to buy that factory and the Ffalda Hotel, before I buy Margam Castle for the family.'

'Just a minute now,' said Twm. 'Who said I was selling them?'

Keeping fit

Ned was reputed to be the best collier in the Ribbon Drift. His friends couldn't understand how he had managed, throughout the years, to work a sixteen inch seam. It was so thin that the colliery was called *The Ribbon*. Ezra Rees, secretary of the Oddfellows Lodge, asked him his secret.

'Is it true that you are keeping fit and thin by eating only pancakes?' he asked.

'Well, it is and it is not true,' Ned replied. 'I never eat anything fatter than a pancake, but the wife doesn't put anything before me, not even a pancake, unless it has been through the mangle!'

The right measurement

William Rees was trying to fill a gap in the railroad leading to the parting where he worked, when the railroad manager appeared.

'I can't understand those blacksmiths – they take no notice of the measurements I've given them,' William said.

'Let's see,' said the manager. 'What measurement did you give them?'

'Two and a half inches, boss,' William said. The boss took out his rule and found the measurement to be exactly right.

'When you order again, don't use figures,' the boss said. 'Simply say the measurements and provide a piece of string or wire to represent it.' When the manager returned to the surface some time later, he was approached by one of the blacksmiths, who said,

'I received this order from William Rees to send a piece of rail, at once with your permission. The measurement is – an *OXO* box in length, and one finger in width.'

First Aid

Wil Charles had been attending a First Aid course and, on his way home from the mine, came across a woman who was bleeding profusely from a wound on the wrist. Wil took out his pay docket and wrapped it around her wrist. Another First Aider asked him what he thought he was doing with such a dirty piece of paper.

'I know exactly what I'm doing,' Wil said. 'I can stop the bleeding with this because there's enough stoppages on it to stop a river!'

Linguistic Oddities

The following are the aftermath of people talking in their second language, English, while thinking in their first language, Welsh.

I can't come tonight because we've got strange people coming here.

• • •

What's the weather going to be like Twm?
   There'll be a fat fog on the mountain tonight, Bob.

• • •

How is your sister? Is she still in bed?
   Oh yes, she's still in bed. But she's standing on her sitting now.

• • •

The Deacon, well versed in the ways of colonialism, decided to give the chapel's weekly announcements in English because a single English visitor was present. He cleared his throat and told the packed chapel,
   'Now we will take the collection,' he said. 'John Parry will go to *hel* this side and William Davies will go to *hel* that side. Please note that the preacher for next Sunday is hanging in the porch . . . Now I'd better leave it at that before I make a muck of it.'

                              (*Hel* is the Welsh word for 'collect')

• • •

The Englishman asked the local butcher if he would kill his pig for him.

'Yes, of course,' was the reply. 'I'm going to kill myself today and I'll come to kill you tomorrow.'

• • •

Giving direction to a lost Englishman . . .

'Go down the lane to the bottom, turn to your right and you will be in Bangor on your head.'

He's still lost!

• • •

Another one received the following enlightenment on his predicament . . .

'Turn left and you'll be right.'

• • •

An old boy from Penmachno was asked,

'Are you married?'

'No, no,' he said, 'I'm still a badger.' His friend was also unmarried, and said,

'I'm a "miss" as well.'

• • •

They are drinking behind hours in there.

• • •

Nain Jones's house was on the main road from Llanelli to the Gower peninsula. After chapel on a Sunday evening, if the weather was fine, she would take her chair and sit on the lawn to watch the traffic and the usual Sunday parade. It was a common sight to see couples on motorbikes going to or returning from the Gower. Nain, being strict chapel, objected to the sight and turned to her next door neighbour who was also sitting on the lawn, saying;

'Look at those girls – their skirts up to their adenoids riding those pavilions.'

• • •

Someone is singing his horn.

• • •

The mechanic, returning the new squire his old tractor, reported;

'Its noise is all right now.'

• • •

An English newcomer wanted to know what was going on in the local chapel. It was a temperance meeting, but he was told;

'It's a sing-song against the beer.'

• • •

Meurig, a country policeman in the Bala area, was called upon to report in court on a fracas between neighbours.

'And who is making these allegations?' the Clerk of the Court demanded.

'I am the allegator,' Meurig replied.

• • •

Many have fallen foul of such linguistic traps when translating as they talk. Such a mental feat as talking one language while thinking in another is beyond the comprehension of monoglots, whatever their language. The following, however, possibly happened to talkers who had simply not engaged the brain before putting the mouth in gear.

We were drilling in granite and it was as hard as rocks!

• • •

As the fly crows.

• • •

Train to Heathrow then a test tube there.

• • •

And then we went over the Pyramids to Spain.

• • •

Whilst explaining the suitability of a concert hall, the commentator noted that:

'The agnostics of the place are excellent.'

• • •

The BBC Sympathy Orchestra.

• • •

The next hymn is by Anon.

Rugby Humour

In spite of its very English origins, rugby has long been adopted as the national sport of Wales. It has been pervaded by the humour of the industrial valleys and, even in lean years for the national team, its following has never faltered. The game became a part of every day existence in many parts of Wales and nothing is celebrated with more vigour than the success of the national team. Parc-yr-Arfau/Cardiff Arms Park became a cathedral during international games, with fervent singing of Welsh hymns by hordes who never darkened the doors of chapel or church. The enthusiasm of some fans is a passion that goes beyond normal day to day affairs, especially when Wales are engaging the arch enemy, England. All seats have been sold well in advance and, on one occasion, Dai Davies couldn't understand why there was an empty seat next to Mr Jones, on his right.

'Yes, said Mr Jones. 'The seat belongs to Mrs Jones.'

'But couldn't she come to the game?' Dai asked.

'No, she couldn't. I'm afraid she died last week.'

'Oh dear, I'm sorry,' Dai said. 'But wouldn't one of your friends have liked Mrs Jones's seat?'

'Oh no,' said Mr Jones. 'My dear, loyal friends are all at Mrs Jones's funeral today.'

Playing for Wales was associated with fame, great esteem and even a certain mystique. It amounted at times to eminence that was at times awesome, and even godly! It is well founded that Woolworth girls curtsied to Barry John, *The King* as he was dubbed, and that mothers used to bring their children to touch him. Alun Richards the writer said that he was a *Church* stand-off because he had plenty of time to do things; he never seemed hurried. Phil Bennett and Cliff Morgan on the other hand were *Chapel* stand-offs – forever trying things and following the ball. *Chapel* or *Church*, their respective styles were just as effective in the course of the many games they played for Wales. So successful did the team become that Frank Keating recalls hearing the radio news in a dingy Fishguard bar, when it was announced that the new Polish Pope had decided against a posh St Peter's coronation, and that he would not wear the priceless Triple Crown of his predecessors. A little man sitting next to him muttered:

'Triple Crown? I s'pose Gareth wouldn't let him borrow it, see.'

Gareth Edwards, voted the greatest rugby player ever during the 1999 Rugby World Cup in Cardiff, was a fitness freak and wonderfully quick witted. Cliff Jones the chairman of selectors came into the hotel foyer where the players were staying. He said to Gareth, who had been suffering from a hamstring niggle or something,

'Fitness test half-past eight tomorrow morning, across the road there. Anyway, how are you feeling?' Gareth's reply was to do twenty summersaults on the hotel carpet, without removing his blazer. The fitness test was deemed unnecessary!

Keith Jarrett had a sensational international debut scoring nineteen points, equalling the then Welsh record, and seemed to beat England single-handed. He had even done this having been selected to play out of his usual position of full-back. Late that night, following a celebration banquet, he arrived at the Cardiff bus station having missed the last bus home. His expenses would certainly not stretch to a taxi home, so he chose the only other option and settled on a bench in the bus station to wait for the first bus home in the morning.

He felt miserable after such a perfect day. However, his luck was in for he was spotted and recognised by the last single deck bus driver. Without hesitation, the star-struck driver decided that he would take Keith home in his bus, special delivery. Keith could not believe his luck, but his heart sank when the inspector rushed out and demanded to know what on earth was going on.

The shaking driver (who stood to lose his job) hurriedly explained and the Inspector immediately ordered them out of the single-decker. He then said;

'Take a double-decker. Mr Jarrett might want to smoke.'

The invincibility of the international fifteen of the 1970's was carried into the individual personalities of the players. When JPR Williams crashed his Ford Capri into a tanker on his way to a Welsh trial, he was shaken but still managed to turn out that afternoon. Tom Bellion, a poet, wrote:

JPR collides with a tanker – the tanker spent a comfortable night in hospital, but is expected to recover!

Bobby Windsor and Tony 'Charlie' Faulkner, the Pontypool players, were taken in for questioning by the police over some 'minor misunderstanding'. They believed that it was important for their accounts of the incident to agree in every detail. They had only the briefest time to prepare but their accounts matched perfectly except for the moment when the cat ran in front of the car!

Bobby said the cat was black. Charlie said it was white! The cat became a very serious stumbling block in the investigation.

'Was the cat black or white?' That was the question posed to Charlie.

'What you have to remember,' he said, 'is that it was a very frosty night!'

Clive Rowlands, the former captain and coach, was famous for his pep talks to the players. Fifteen times he would bellow:

'What are we going to do?' Each time, he would point to a player who was expected to bellow back equally as loudly, 'WIN'. But when John Lloyd of Bridgend played, he was allowed to shout, 'Eat 'em'.

Then, Rowlands would embark upon his monologue.

'You are going out to win for your country. For Wales. For your dada. For the mam that nursed you. For your wife. For your sweetheart. For your Auntie Gladys. For that tart you met on Saturday! For the man on the bus this morning.

A new cap heard this for the first time and was awestruck but, after playing for twenty minutes, he turned to his pal in the scrum and said.

'Hey, wait a mo. I haven't got an Auntie Gladys. And that tart on Saturday said she didn't want to see me ever again!'

Another great pep talker was Ray Gravell. The players were all steamed up and ready to go out to face the enemy, when he called them all back. With tears streaming down into his sandy beard, he said to them: 'Boys, I've got a telegram here that I want to read to you – *Best wishes to my son* it says. *All my love*, and do you know who signed it?

From Mam and Shamrock! Do you know who Shamrock is, boys? The . . . cat! The . . . cat . . . sent us a telegram!'

Ray Prosser, the famous prop forward, disliked flying. When his friend asked him why, the reply was, 'Because my legs aren't long enough.'

'What d'you mean?'

'I like to have one foot on the ground.'

'But you're willing to travel by sea, and the ship could sink,' his friend said.

'I can swim a bit, but I can't fly at all!' was the reasoning.

Such reasoning might be behind the rituals before every match, which were full of superstitions. Ray Gravell ate soft centres! Brian Thomas of Neath would eat a pound of grapes for breakfast while Merfyn Davies would have a great fry-up at ten o'clock, followed by a piece of fish and a cup of tea for his pre-match lunch at one o'clock. Delme Thomas had to have a huge steak washed down by a pint of milk – any conversation referring to this practise was usually ended by the big man saying 'Now let's get this straight, are you complaining about the way I play, or what? JPR, the doctor, would eat nothing all day except a few slices of toast and honey, while Dai Watkins, Ray Prosser and the muscle packed hard-men of the Pont-y-pŵl front row did or could not eat anything whatsoever. To be fair, the 'Poolers' maintained that the reason for their not eating was that a hungry lion was a much more dangerous animal than one that was fully fed. Probably the strangest though was Max Wiltshire of Aberafon who insisted on having his curry and rice, and made sure of its availability by carrying with him little packets of 'Vesta'.

The name of that particularly offensive food-like

substance reminds one of Colin Howe, the Cardiff prop who had a riotous sense of humour. After a match against the boys of a church school in England, he engaged one of the lads in conversation.

'Coming for a pint then?' Colin enquired.

'Oh no, sir, we've got vespers,' the lad replied.

'Oh don't bother with those old bikes. Come on the bus with us!' advised Colin.

Tickets to actually see a match were, and often still are, like gold dust. A week before one Wales *v* England match, a small add appeared in the *South Wales Echo*:

'Desperately wanted – Ticket for the Match. Offers Rolls Royce car in exchange.'

The next day, a reply appeared;

'Will yesterday's advertiser please state what year is the Rolls Royce.'

Before the game, Gareth Edwards was summoned to Buckingham Palace to receive his MBE. A cartoon by *Gren* appeared in the *Echo*, showing two pithead workers reading the headline: QUEEN SEES GARETH AT PALACE. The caption read; 'Amazing the lengths some people go to try and get a ticket.'

Only one 'civilian' was allowed in the dressing room, this being the physiotherapist Gerry Lewis. One of his jobs was to rush out if an injury occurred that needed his bucket of 'good Welsh tap water' and a magic sponge. It had to be Welsh tap water because . . . 'plain cold water does no good. It compresses the wound, freezes it.'

Lewis was very aware of the solemnity of each occasion. He would greet every player with a handshake and lowered eyes, and then hand over the new gleaming scarlet shirt that he had pressed and folded with the motif as the centrepiece. He gave Gareth Edwards more than fifty shirts and he would unfailingly kiss the feathers on the badge and then kiss Lewis on both cheeks. Barry John received his silently and then gave him a hug. Charlie Faulkner used to throw his in the air and say 'Effing 'eck, I've got another one'!

When the team flew to Paris they were expected to attend film shows. Lewis, being a highly cultured man, used to creep away and try to catch an opera. His Grandfather had been a minister of religion and Lewis inherited some of that saintliness. In his famous little black bag he carried two sizes of Elastoplast, bandages, Vaseline, Deep-Heat, smelling salts and a Bible. In his own words, he was 'never without it. Our Welsh boys are . . . for some reason quick to be homesick and . . . my Bible came in handy.' On one occasion when he was in charge of the Welsh 'B' international team playing at Lourdes, he announced that the following morning he was going to attend mass at the Basilica. His invitation to any team members to join him was met with an universal response of 'get stuffed!' The following morning nineteen out of a squad of twenty-one joined him.

The magic of the seventies could and did not last. But rugby continues to inhabit the imagination of school children, club members and people of all ages, and both sexes, across Wales. It is by now a far more 'national' game than it was in the time of Gareth, Barry, Phil and company. It has always produced characters around whom stories abound, some printable and many unmentionable.

Dai Hayward once claimed that prop forwards have considerable wit in addition to their weight. Since this assertion has been severely doubted in many quarters, he went on to cite J.D. Evans, an international prop, who was merrily puffing his cigarette as he watched Dai warming-up. When Dai told him off for smoking before an important game, he received the answer, 'Look boyo, you warm-up your way, and I'll warm-up mine!'

During the game he took Dai to one side and said that Dai was pushing incorrectly on his follow-in-leg. Dai did not understand what he meant. In the end, Evans said;

'Dai, we'll compromise. You do my running and I'll do your pushing!'

Dai was at one time working for a Hereford cider firm, where his boss was Glan Williams, a one time great rugby player. Dai was captain of Cardiff and was due to lead his team against Swansea, who were captained by Gwyn Lewis, another fine player.

Dai received a memo from Glan Williams on the morning of the match, saying,

'Dear David, do not hit Gwyn today. Yours sincerely, Glan.'

Gwyn was far bigger than Dai but the note implied that the villain was Dai. After the match Gwyn drew Dai aside and told him that he had also received a similar memo!

A prop forward without too much of Hayward's wit was a South African in his first term at Oxford, who had been given a place in the first fifteen for the pre-Varsity match against Cardiff. The team travelled to Chepstow, where they stayed the night. As they approached Chepstow the captain stood up and asked them all to check their passports. The South African claimed that he didn't know a passport was required to cross into Wales. He was warned that he would never get past the customs so it was decided that he should hide in the boot of the coach. Soon afterwards one of the players, with a thick Welsh accent, walked around the coach and banged on the boot demanding to know what was in there. He was assured that it was only rugby kit, and the coach continued. The Cardiff players were told of the incident and asked to play along as they were going to do the same on the way back. And they did!

Cliff Davies, one of the 'mules of Kenfig Hill' was a great storyteller. He was also a singer and a real entertainer who had the knack of inventing memorable phrases and sayings. He was also a part-time undertaker and had many funereal tales to tell. Bill Tamplin the Welsh lock forward asked Cliff how things were in the undertaking business.

'Middling Tamp, not bad,' was the reply.

'How much are you charging for coffins these days?'

'Nothing special . . . fourteen guineas in fact.'

'That's a bit steep, isn't it? I saw one advertised in the paper for twelve pounds, and a pleasure to lie in!'

'Well Tamp, take it if you like it, but let me warn you, pitch pine it'll be, and your arse'll be through it in six months!'

Prior to the 1950 tour, he surprised Bleddyn Williams and Jack Matthews on a shopping trip down Oxford Street. He asked them to accompany him to a shop where he was going to obtain some shirts, and explained that his uncle was the boss. Williams and Matthews assumed that the uncle was in charge of the shirt department when they entered John Lewis's, which was a considerable establishment. They were led to a lift and taken to the top floor, and were then ushered into a long posh room where Cliff's uncle sat at a huge mahogany desk. He was the big man for the whole store, not just the shirt department!

A great fuss was made of Cliff and then his uncle asked what he could do for him.

'Some shirts,' Cliff replied. A button was pressed and the shirt buyer appeared.

'I want a dozen shirts for my nephew!' the uncle ordered.

'Certainly sir!' said the buyer and turned to Cliff to enquire about the collar size.

'Nineteen and a half,' Cliff said. The buyer visibly paled. They didn't have shirts with collars of that size and since Cliff was leaving in two days, the shirts had to be made overnight.

And so it came to be that Cliff from Kenfig Hill, or Mynydd Cynffig to give its Welsh name, was the only member of the 1950 Lion's squad wearing hand made shirts!

Cliff, being from a mining background, still managed to overcome the prejudice that there could have come from the many ex-public school and university members of the squad. At the end of the 1950 Lions tour of New Zealand and Australia, Cliff became sentimental about parting from his friends. They started talking about holidays.

'When the tour is over, come down to Kenfig Hill for a bit,' Cliff said. 'There's more history attached to Kenfig Hill than any other city in the world!' The elegant Peter Kininmouth, captain of Scotland and Oxford sniggered, and like a flash Cliff added . . . 'Barring Jerusalem of course!'

He once told the tale of the young nonconformist preacher who came to minister in Mynydd Cynffig. The minister was ordained in the chapel on the Thursday night and played for the local rugby team the following Saturday. As Cliff was leaving the chapel service on the Sunday, someone asked him what he thought of the new preacher. The verdict was;

'I've got to admit that he's powerful in prayer, but bloody hopeless in the lineout.'

Clive Rowlands is another with a very ready tongue allied to a very sharp brain. He relates a story about Dai Morris, colliery blacksmith and hard as nails backrow forward. Dai loved horse racing and had a horse of his own which he kept on top of a hill overlooking Cwm Rhondda. Dai was in the dressing room with the others when Clive entered to give his pep performance. Barry John was, as usual, looking out of the window. Dai Morris had his elbows on his knees, hands clasped over his ears.

'Boys,' Clive said, 'look at Dai Morris now. His concentration on this game against England is an example to everyone . . . I want you to concentrate like Dai . . . '

And the object of his admiration said, 'Shut up Clive, I'm trying to listen to the two-fifteen from Catterick!'

Another time, Rowlands was having an intense meeting with Brian Thomas.

'At scrum-half they have a bloke called Trevor Whittle,' he said, as if the man had a criminal record. 'Might even call him a friend because we were at Cambridge together, but all that is in the past! We concentrate on him and when he comes off the field I want him to look as if he's been sunbathing in the Bahamas with a string vest on!'

Clive Rowlands still has much to say on the state of the game in Wales, sometimes saying more in jest than many others say in the course of the entire season. During the

1999/2000 season, much was made of Rob Howley's loss of form, and especially the slowness of his pass from the base of the scrum. It was decided when Wales were struggling through a miserable inaugural Six rather than Five Nations tournament, that Howley should be dropped. Rowlands was informed of his replacement at a meeting, and expressed some surprise that the new national scrum half was to be an old one with an even slower pass from the base of the scrum, namely Rupert Moon. He was told that Moon had already worked wonders in the dressing room, that the mood had lightened considerably, and that the boys were laughing at his jokes. Rowlands's immediate off the cuff comment was;

'Why didn't they go all the way and pick Owen Money?' (who is a comedian on the South Wales club circuit and a BBC radio presenter who laughs a lot).

Rupert Moon was born and bred in the English Midlands, but became a naturalized Welshman having studied at Swansea University and played for Llanelli for many years. But Tony Copsey was the first Englishman to qualify for Wales having also made a career for himself with the Scarlets in Llanelli. He once blatantly chinned Neil Francis, a fellow big second row player, in a line-out during an Ireland/Wales match in Dublin. Ieuan Evans, in his first championship match as captain, pleaded with the referee not to send Copsey off. In the dressing room, after the match, Copsey expressed his gratitude to Ieuan. As an Essex lad from Romford he had *Made in England* tattooed on his backside! When he thanked Ieuan, he was told, 'just make sure you get another tattoo on the other cheek . . . one that says *Refined in Wales*'!

Homely Humour

Humour comes in all shapes and sizes. The following are a collection from various sources on differing themes, the main qualifying factor being that they should not offend anybody apart from the very thin skinned.

Religious summit

The vicar's wife invited the wife of the Methodist preacher to a river bank picnic with the intention of comparing strategies in halting the decline in attendance at their husbands respective establishments. The 'summit' occurred on a sunny June afternoon on the banks of Afon Conwy. The six year old son of the vicar was soon bored stiff, and asked his mother if he and the five year old preacher's daughter might go swimming. There were no bathing costumes, but it was decided that the children could bathe in the nude.

When the vicar's wife arrived home, her son rushed to report the afternoon's events to his busy father, shouting merrily:

'It was brilliant dad. But I didn't know there was such a difference between Church and Chapel!'

Faded goods

An Anglesey man from Llanerchymedd visited London for the first time. In the confusion of travelling on the tube, he lost his hat. He found his way to an important hat shop and the assistant brought out four hats for him to try. He chose one and was told that it would cost him £5.

'Good heavens!' the man exclaimed. 'Back home, I could get one exactly like that for thirty shillings!'

'That may well be so!' replied the assistant. 'But we have large windows here, full of hats. When they fade we send them to places like Llanerchymedd where they are sold very cheaply!'

The Welshman bought the hat with some reluctance and as he was leaving, the assistant said, 'It is quite a coincidence! My wife comes from Llanerchymedd. You may have known her. She was Ellen Jones who lived at The Mill!'

'Know her!' the man replied. 'She was a very pretty girl. I took her out many a time!' And after a pause he added, 'When things get a bit faded in Llanerchymedd . . . we send them to London!'

Oh my God

Dai and Blodwen had been married for many years but had no children. Dai worked at the local factory; Blodwen stayed looking after the home.

One day, when she visited the doctor, he told her she was pregnant. Blodwen was delighted and phoned Dai at the factory.

'Ullo!' Dai said.

'I'm pregnant!' Blodwen shouted.

There was dead silence.

'Dai! I tell you that I'm pregnant! Say something!' shouted Blodwen.

'Who's speaking?' Dai asked.

Telling tales

A Pembrokeshire vicar was constantly embarrassed by his two lads swearing in public. He decided that the matter had to be resolved and asked his policeman friend to have a word with them.

The policeman came one day and told them, in a guarded manner, that he had heard that they swore too much and that if they continued, he would have to do something about it.

The boys used to stock the bird table every morning without fail, but the next morning neither of the boys made any effort to feed their feathered friends. Their father asked them why they were on strike, and was told by the eldest boy;

'No way will we feed those little bastards after they've been telling tales about us!'

Black magic

One of the quarrymen had fallen and the wound had left a scar on his forehead. He was in the local pub one night when the doctor came in. He asked the doctor if he could treat the scar, and then how much it would cost.

'Three guineas,' the doctor said.

'Wil,' said the quarryman, 'give the good doctor three bottles of Guinness please. He's going to treat my scar!'

No, no Mr Jones

The committee in charge of improving facilities in the local park was in session, and the councillors were making suggestions.

'Why not have a gondola on the lake?' one asked.

'Indeed,' said the chairman, 'why not have two? We could breed from them.'

'Hang on now,' said another. 'Who's going to feed them?'

Oh no Miss Jones

A young woman was going on a trip to London when she should have been at work. When she arrived at Cardiff station she decided to phone her employer and tell him that she was in bed with flu. As she was explaining the symptoms at some length, the station announcer said loudly,

'The next train to arrive at Cardiff station will be . . . '

Go to IKEA

The University of Wales wrote to several local authorities to support the effort to establish another Chair. One authority, after a great deal of discussion, decided to offer the sum of £200. But Councillor Bill Williams got up and said;

'I suggest that the University be advised to buy a much cheaper chair.'

U-boat, U-boat!

Soon after the Second World War, Enoch became a familiar figure around Dyffryn Ogwen with his pony and cart, selling herring.

'How much are they?' Mrs Jones asked.

'Ten pennies each,' was the reply.

'My goodness,' said Mrs Jones. 'Expensive they are, and so thin!'

'So would you be woman,' Enoch replied, 'if you had been avoiding submarines for six years.'

Never forget your Welsh

Enoch used to walk up and down the streets of Bethesda followed by his pony, and he used his considerable vocal prowess to advertise his wares. On one occasion, he was loudly shouting;

'FRESH FISH, FRESH FISH . . . ' as he walked. He was interrupted by an even louder woman, shouting;

'Gweidda yn Gymraeg y Lembo!' (Shout in Welsh you idiot)

There was a moment of total silence, and then Enoch resumed;

'FISH FRESH, FISH FRESH . . . '

Misdiagnosis

One of the workmen in the food cabin at the Penrhyn slate quarry told the others that the cobbler had been taken to hospital.

'What's wrong with him?' someone asked.

'Gallstones.'

'Get off! He's never worked in a quarry . . . he was a cobbler!'

It's for you

Nain Jones was greatly excited when a phone was installed in her house. But she had never used one and was petrified that the thing might ring when she was alone in the house. Ring it did however, and she finally plucked up the courage to answer it. It was her sister, Mary, asking whether Nain had found an umbrella that had been left during Mary's visit, two days earlier?

'Wait there now!' granny said. She put the phone down and fetched the umbrella, held it up to the phone and shouted, 'Is this the one Mary?'

Touch-up sir?

A young woman from Llanfair Pwllgwyngyll got into her car to get to Kwik Save. She failed to start the engine and called on her husband to help, but he was taking too long so she decided to walk the half-mile to the store. When she returned she saw his legs sticking out from under the car. She dropped her bag and playfully ran her hand up his leg before disappearing into the house . . . to find her husband sitting in the kitchen!

The last word, always!

Lloyd George was being heckled while speaking about home rule for Wales.

'And what about hell?' the heckler shouted.

'Every man to his own country!' was the reply.

Another silly question

The Revd J.C. Jones answered the door to a young woman.

'Will you marry me, your reverence?' the young woman enquired.

'Of course,' he replied. 'But had you not better see the nest first?'

Rats to you

John Morris's farm in Dyffryn Nantlle was overrun with rats. He went to the local Post Office to phone Jones' Ironmongers in Caernarfon. He explained his problem to the ironmonger and asked if there were any suitable traps.

'Yes, of course!' said Jones. 'Would you like me to send them to you?'

'Oh yes indeed,' Morris answered. 'That would be infinitely easier than me sending the rats to you!'

Ask a silly question

A little boy was playing football in the street, and crying.

'And what can the matter be, then?' asked the passing minister.

'My father and mother are quarrelling,' the child replied.

'Oh dear,' the kindly minister said. 'And who might be your father then?'

'That's what they're quarrelling about,' was the reply.

Always look on the bright side of life

An old lady in Cricieth bought dozens of sympathy cards. The young man serving her asked whether she needed so many.

'Oh yes!' was the adamant reply. 'Nothing like being prepared, is there?'

Anything you can do

Twm and Dylan were in the same class at primary school, and were always trying to score off each other. They had compared the number of sheep their respective farms grazed. They had compared the horsepower of their respective tractors and the merits of a *John Deere* over a *Massey Ferguson*, or vice versa. They had even compared the virility of Twm's Limousine bull compared to Dylan's Charolais.

Today, it was Taid.

'Both my grandfathers are dead,' said Dylan.

'One of mine is dead,' Twm replied. 'And the other is going to die!'

What a waste

Owen Rowlands, blacksmith and chapel goer, had to travel from Trefor to Llanaelhaearn for his pint. Sometimes he did this three times a week. One night after he had returned home and was leaning on the front gate, the Revd W.D. Evans saw a beer bottle sticking out of his pocket.

'I am very surprised to see that you are a beer drinker, Owen,' said the preacher.

'Oh, very seldom indeed,' was the reply. 'In fact, Jos next door was parched and I offered to go and share a bottle with him.'

'In that case,' the good Revd suggested, 'pour away your half.'

'Can't do that,' Owen said. 'Mine is the bottom half!'

Was your father a donkey?

A husband and wife were quarrelling in their car. They came across a mule on the road and the creature refused to move.

'That thing is as obstinate as you!' the husband said. 'He must be related to you.'

'Only through marriage!' was the reply.

No Smoking

The Revd was travelling in a non-smoking compartment with his pipe in his mouth.

'Here!' the young woman passenger said. 'You're not allowed to smoke in here!'

'I'm not smoking.'

'You've got your pipe in your mouth,' she objected.

'Yes,' he replied. 'And I have boots on my feet, but I'm not walking, am I?'

Cheep at half the price
An old lady was selling cracked eggs at half price at Llanelli market. A customer asked her to crack her a dozen.

A great loss
The headmaster of a popular Welsh medium secondary school died and there was considerable speculation as to who would succeed him. The crematorium was busy and the dead man was awaiting burial for a long time. One of the would-be applicants buttonholed the chairman of the education committee and asked 'Would you have any objection to my taking the place of the headmaster?'

''No,' replied the chairman, 'I don't mind at all. Go and see the undertaker, but be quick.'

Us and them
A shipwrecked Welshman was marooned on a desert island. When a passing tanker picked him up seven years later, the captain and crew were amazed at the man's ingenuity. The proud Robin Croesor took them around the island showing his house, workshop, hydroelectric generator and two chapels.

'Why two chapels?' asked the fascinated captain.

'That's the one I don't go to,' was the reply.

Not tonight Josephine
The night porter in a Llandudno hotel was shocked when a guest from a visiting ladies cerdd dant choir came down stairs at the witching hour dressed in a revealing pink negligée. He tapped her on her shoulder and asked;

'What on earth are you doing coming down here

dressed like that?' The soprano jumped and blearily gazed at the porter, saying;

'Oh, I'm sorry, I'm a somnambulist.'

'I don't care what chapel you belong to,' said the porter. 'You better get back to bed before I report you to your conductor.'

Him and her

A young lady of seven was demonstrating her linguistic ability to her mother and older brother. She had been reading about pairs of animals, like Noah, and was listing both sexes of each species.

'*Bull* is male, *cow* is female,' she said. She then went on to list *sheep* and *ram*, *hen* and *cockrel*, *sow* and *boar*, etc. etc.

Her older brother didn't think much of this display so, hoping he might catch her out, he asked,

'If you're so clever, what's the female of *dog*?'

'*Bitch*' was the instant reply. 'And the male's a *bastard*!'

Choir Humour

If rugby, coal pit-heads and sheep infested slate-tip covered mountainsides are some of the idiosyncratic pictures that many foreigners have of Wales, then the sound of our singing surely completes the album. Wales has been called, amongst a host of other things, the land of song. This is generally untrue since most Welshmen, and women, can't sing – it just seems that we all can. But this postage stamp on a map of Europe, and large pinhead on a map of the world, hosts annually the largest cultural event in Europe, and probably the world, that is wholly dedicated to youth – and the Urdd movement continues to grow and gain ground in the country, eighty years and more after it's inception. This country's comparatively small population has through the ages produced a high proportion of professional singers. The singing at Cardiff Arms Parc, when the chapels were losing their hold on the population and while the population still remembered the hymns, raised the small hairs on the backs of the Welsh players – heaven only knows what effect it had on visiting teams. The most obvious sign was that the crowds forgetting their hymns coincided with the Welsh national side forgetting its habit of winning.

Welsh choirs have long taken their sounds to all the inhabited continents of the world. These have always included very successful and accomplished female and mixed voice choirs but, for some reason, it is the male voice choirs that have caught the imagination abroad. Most towns and many villages have their own male voice choirs and some even have two – and even hamlets in agricultural areas manage to maintain their own four part harmony male voice ensembles. There are of course, like in boxing, divisions within the choir ranks ranging from the heavyweights to the lightweights, mainly based on the number of singers. And critics will also tell you that there are one or two sublime choirs, some good ones, some that are mediocre; there are some bad choirs and there are quite a few abysmal ones.

What follows is an account of the lighter side of being a member of a male voice choir.

Encore

A renowned male choir, basking in its self-acclaimed international reputation, was coming to the end of an evening's performance in a village near Merthyr Tudful. To end the evening's programme they sang the famous song *Myfanwy*, the most famous composition by Joseph Parry, the most famous musical son of Merthyr. At the end of the rendition, a little man in the front row stood up and waved his arms vigorously, shouting 'Again! Again!' The choir's musical director bowed proudly and the choir sang *Myfanwy* again. Once more the man stood on his feet shouting 'Again! Again!'

So the choir sang it a third time, at the end of which the man was once more on his feet crying, with even more passion, 'Again! Again!' So *Myfanwy* was sung for an unprecedented fourth time and still the man was shouting 'Again! Again!'

The musical director turned to the man and said, 'I'm sorry sir, but we couldn't possibly sing it again.' And the little man replied,

'Oh yes you will – and you will sing it until you get it right!'

Get on with it

The same choir was performing in a small village hall in west Wales, the concert to commence at seven o'clock. With a few minutes to go, the musical director peeped through the curtain to find a solitary male sitting at the rear of the hall. He waited another ten minutes and there was just that one man. The musical director turned to the choir and said, 'Gentlemen there is but one man in the audience. But we will honour our commitment and perform in the usual way.' He stepped onto the front of the stage and said,

'Sir, although you appear to be the audience this evening, we will perform for you as if the hall was packed to capacity.' The man replied,

'Well don't be long. I'm the caretaker and I want to lock up.'

Second chance

At the cremation of a choir president the hymn *Gwahoddiad*, containing the lines *Mi glywaf dyner lais Yn galw arnaf i*, (I hear Thy welcome voice, That calls me Lord to Thee) was sung. During the hymn one of the second tenors, who had a heart condition, collapsed in a heap. The choir kept singing to the end of the hymn but as soon as the final *Amen* had been sung, a doctor from among the mourners attended to the unfortunate chorister. An ambulance was called and he was taken to hospital.

One of the paramedics was heard to say to him,

'This is the first man who has ever been wheeled *out* of this place!'

DRUNKARDS!

A choir gave a concert in a small village near Salisbury and were joined by a local band with which they had a long association. The choir were to sing 'March of the Peers' from *Iolanthe*, accompanied by the band.

On the day of the performance, the choir spent three hours before the rehearsal at the local pub. As the rehearsal time approached the conductor of the band called in the bar to ask the choir to attend the rehearsal. He was a very nervous individual and, when he saw the state of some choristers, beat a hasty retreat!

The rehearsal, when it was eventually held, was a complete shambles until the choir's stage-master called for attention. He ordered the choir to dress from the right and face the right way. Two of the bass immediately fell off the stage into the wings! One was concussed, the other badly shaken. The rehearsal was abandoned and the bandmaster was by this time a nervous wreck!

After several cups of black coffee the choir performed superbly and received a standing ovation. The audience demanded that they sang the piece again and again.

The moral of this story might be that Welsh choirs sing better after the larynx has been well oiled. Even so, the rule now with this particular choir is . . .

'NO ALCOHOL BEFORE PUBLIC PERFORMANCE'!

Toast

A chorister had performed over fifty concerts with his choir and was well known for his *Pedro the Fisherman* and *Goin' Home*. The latter was a setting of the slow movement from Dvorak's Symphony No. 9 *(The New World)* and became the theme music for the Hovis adverts.

Goin' Home was often the climax of his performance, during which he made a stage-left exit while sustaining a very long note, holding out his left hand as he looked at the audience until he finally disappeared.

The conductor decided that the song might benefit from a different ending. As the erstwhile singer left the stage in his usual manner, a Hovis loaf was placed in his outstretched hand. He continued singing and walked off! It was never known whether he appreciated the new arrangement because nothing was ever said about the incident!

The language of heaven

A south Wales choir was on a visit to Canada and the USA and were treated with great affection everywhere they went. Gwilym and his wife were sitting at the dining table with their Canadian hosts when the host asked . . .

'Do you speak Welsh, Gwilym?' Without thinking, Gwilym replied,

'Yes, a little.'

'Wonderful!' said their host, 'We would be deeply honoured if you would say grace in Welsh.'

Not wanting to appear rude and silly, Gwilym put his hands together, invited the others to join him and said:

'Oes gafr eto, oes heb ei godro, Tydi a Roddaist, Gwahoddiad, Ein Tad yr hwn wyt yn y nefoedd . . . Amen.'

The host shed a tear and said,

'Thank you so much Gwilym! That was very touching . . . We shall treasure those beautiful words for ever!'

The chorister's wife was also in tears. She was nearly falling off her chair in silent hysterics because Gwilym had recited two lines of a Welsh folk song, the titles of two Welsh hymns and the first line of The Lord's Prayer!

Spiritual men

A choir from a small town in south Wales was performing in Manchester and, during their spare time, the choristers visited one of the big stores. As they went up the escalator to the upper floor they started to sing *We are Climbing Jacob's Ladder* in four part harmony. The other shoppers were greatly startled, but the choir was disappointed not to meet Gabriel on the upper floor!

OBE

Moriah Chapel had an organ that had to be pumped by hand. Dan Evans was the only person allowed anywhere near the pump, and he merrily pumped away at all kinds of music. The usual hymn tunes were not much of a challenge; but when the chapel choir decided to tackle 'The Hallelujah Chorus' from Handel's *Messiah*, it was a very different business altogether!

Even so, he still managed a smile in the middle of such a demanding piece and for his marathon exploit, became known locally as Dan Evans O.B.E: (Organ Blower Evans).

Bright bunch

When choirs plan concert tours, they also plan some sightseeing around the singing. This explains why so many choirs visit New England during the famous *fall*. One choir landed at Toronto Airport and were then bussed over to Buffalo on the shores of Lake Erie where other coaches with U.S.A. drivers were waiting for them. They boarded one of the coaches and at the entrance was a message saying:

'Your driver is Earl Robinson: safe, reliable and courteous', and there was a photograph of a very big

Caucasian gentleman.

Other members of the choir boarded a second coach which also had a message at the entrance:

'Your driver is James F Jordan: safe, reliable and courteous', and there was a photograph of a large black gentleman. When James Jordan appeared from the fast food outlet he greeted his passengers with a resonant 'Howdy folks!' All he got in reply were a few non-committal grunts so he sat down in the driver's seat and thought that he had a really bright bunch on his hands. He was about to press the starting button when, at a pre-arranged signal, the choir burst into a lusty rendering of the Negro spiritual *Roll, Jordan, Roll*! Mr Jordan sprang from his seat and his great bulk shook with laughter.

At the next food stop he was heard telling the other drivers, 'On ma coach ah has ma own song!'

What's in a name?

At the famous Massed Male Voice Festival of a 1,000 Voices in the Albert Hall, in 1984, the star of the show was Sir Harry Secombe, who had just returned from the West Indies where he had suffered a stroke.

During the afternoon rehearsal Harry was in cracking form and nearly drove the man who was in charge of timing the show out of his mind. At one time he burst two buttons on his trousers and demanded that someone do emergency repairs. But he rehearsed his two songs, *Swansea Town* and *We'll Keep a Welcome in the Hillsides*, superbly.

Before he left the microphone he said, 'I know all these wonderful lads rather well, you know. In fact, I know them all by name!' He turned to the massed ranks with his back to the auditorium and yelled, 'Dai Jones!'

All one thousand choristers roared back, 'What do you want?'

When this was repeated at the actual concert to an audience of 6,000 people, it brought the house down!

Memory lapses
Barry's misguided wife was delighted that he had decided to join the local Male Voice Choir.

'I'm so glad you won't be drinking and playing darts until midnight every Friday.' she said. 'Now you will be with those tidy boys of the Male Voice!'

After his very first appearance with the choir, Barry got so drunk that he fell asleep in a ditch on his way home. When he woke up the following morning his tuxedo was covered in snail traces. Eventually, he reached a telephone booth and rang his wife to come and get him.

There is reason to believe that he was still not quite thinking straight because he forgot to tell her where he was, and he also forgot that she couldn't drive!

Another forgetful chorister turned up at a concert wearing the usual dark suit, a bow tie and white shirt . . . but also a Fair Isle pullover . . . and bedroom slippers!

Ve haf vays of making you pronounce, Ja
Whilst rehearsing a wordy piece of male voice choir drivel called *Italian Salad*, the conductor was emphasising the importance of correct pronunciation of the words. One phrase needed quick, sharp tongue movements for *Tra Tara Ra Ta Ta Ta*, and he joked that he ought to be surrounded by ninety sets of false teeth if the choir were to pronounce the words correctly.

The following evening one chorister visited his local and asked his older mates for a loan of any spare sets of false teeth! He arrived at the next rehearsal with a plastic bag full of dentures! As the choir started to sing *Italian Salad*, he lowered his hand into the bag and when the right moment came, a handful of second-hand false teeth flew in the direction of the conductor, bouncing all over the wooden classroom floor!

The choristers were nearly choking as they attempted to sing, but the conductor didn't even flinch and continued with the music.

Dog gone!
On a choir's visit to San Francisco in 1990 one of the choristers, Rhys the postman, was suffering badly from jet lag. He was being hosted by a husband and wife in the El Cerito area of the city and found at three o'clock in the morning that he could not sleep, so decided to take the family dog for a walk. He returned to the house at half-past eight and was upset to find that the dog was distressed! Every time the dog heard his voice, he ran to hide. While most of the choristers had walked the Golden Gate bridge, Rhys had walked the whole bay! A special shirt was made for him giving an account of his 'walkie'.

George and Mildred
A choir was to give a concert at the Plymouth Guild Hall. They were met by the organiser and local residents, who were to give them a traditional Cornish Sunday lunch. Every choir member was allocated to a host and told that they had to be back by two o'clock.

At the allotted hour two choir members were missing.

They arrived a few minutes before the choir went on stage, windswept and harassed.

It appeared that the host, who had given the impression that he owned a Mercedes, in fact had a motor-bike and sidecar! The two had argued about who should ride in the sidecar and who should ride pillion: it made little difference, for both appeared with their hair standing on end.

When a man has got to go . . .

At a concert in a Llanelli chapel, the male voice choir took its place on the gallery near the organ. There were only two doors, both at the front of the chapel leading to the upstairs gallery. During the performance, one chorister was 'taken short' and was in urgent need of the toilet facilities. He made eyes at the section leader that he had to leave the stage. He remembered how he had entered the building, but now saw another door by the side of the organ, which he assumed would lead to the toilets. Imagine his embarrassment when, in full view of an amused packed audience, he struggled in vain to open a false door!

Oh what a night

A choir was on its first overseas tour to West Germany in 1975, the choristers being hosted by the residents of a village called Laudenbach, about ten miles from Mannheim. On the first day out on a coach tour, one of the older choristers in the first bass section complained to his fellow choristers about the lack of bedding sheets at his residence. It turned out that he had never seen a continental quilt before and had unbuttoned the cover of the quilt and had slept inside the cover, thinking that it was a sleeping bag!

Hot stuff

A choir was in its first television recording session for HTV in Culverhouse Cross in Cardiff. They were to back a Welsh pop singer in an atmospheric song called *Y Cwm*. On the set, various lighting and special effects had been set up for the actual 'take'. As they came to their big moment, mist was being blown onto the set. Members of the bottom bass (at the far left) were seen closing ranks and moving towards the middle of the choir, whispering quietly, but loudly enough for everyone to hear, 'Ma tân ma!' (There's a fire here!).

Don't follow me, I'm lost too

At the end of a first class tour of Canada in 1990, a choir was embarking on a ferry at Sydney, Vancouver Island, to return to Seattle for the plane to Heathrow. As the departure time drew near, the treasurer and his wife, who had slept late, were the only ones missing from the group. Sydney has three daily ferries: one goes to Vancouver; another goes round the islands; and a third goes to Seattle. The group embarked on the correct ferry but when the treasurer and his wife arrived, in their panic they rushed on to the ferry that was going back to Vancouver! As it set sail, five minutes earlier than the Seattle ferry, the two of them searched the decks for the rest of the group. To make things worse, the treasurer was at the time wearing a peaked cap with the words, 'I'm their leader! Which way did they go?'

Holy Smoke

On a bright Sunday morning in a neat Canadian church, the large visiting Male Voice Choir had sent a body of singers along to join in the service. What is more, to the church elders' pleasure, they donned the long blue surplices of the church and agreed to the request to sing *Myfanwy*. In the respectful silence, as the choir were feathering through the soft passages, a haze was seen to assemble around the figure of a substantially built baritone in the back row, developing gradually into a gentle billowing cloud – his fire retardant surplice had encountered an electric fire behind him! Totally oblivious of his threatened annihilation, he continued to sing with half-closed eyes, lost in the emotion of the piece, until the smoke alerted the others. A chorus of coughing ended the incident.

Rise, Rise the Merry Lark

At a farmhouse in the West Country, after a long concert and even longer post-concert celebration, two extremely weary choristers gratefully climbed into bed in a small room at the back of the farmhouse. The choir had been 'hosted' by the local choral society of which the farmer was a member.

The room was spartan but clean – with a low ceiling, tiny window and bare board floor. The large feather bed filled the room, and in their exhausted state was the most welcome sight in the world. Putting out the light, they sank immediately into the arms of Morpheus.

But at half-past five precisely, the peace exploded with a shattering and sustained roar, the room filled with smoke and the bed began lurching from side to side. The

farmer had forgotten that the ploughman was to start ploughing that morning, and the tractor was stored directly beneath the bedroom!

Duw Yw Fy Mugail – (Do You Vamegyle?)

The following was written by R.G. Mainwaring, a former member of Côr Meibion y Dyfnant (Dunvant Male Coir):

It was written somewhere that an Englishman pronouncing the Welsh language is 'like a man with a mouthful of scalding chips trying to answer the phone'. This might be an uncharitable illustration, but is sufficiently near the truth to be at least recognisable. The fact is that, brought up to speak a tongue which can be enunciated perfectly well whilst gripping a pipe between the teeth, the 'language of heaven' must come as a heck of a shaker to them. It follows therefore that any Englishman who, voluntarily and of his own free will, elects to become a member of a Welsh choir thus exposing himself to the full rigours of 'yr hen iaith', is either inordinately partial to choral music, or not right in the head.

Anyway these were the sentiments running through my head during one celebrated 'afterglow' in the Midlands of England. Mr Bevan, our *unterkapellmeister*, had taken us through a fairly comprehensive programme in the bar, and the singing had reached the inevitable point in the proceedings when the local brand of bitter begins to affect its tonal equilibrium and poetic emphasis. Mr Bevan, recognising death's scaly hand, had called for one last assault on *Sanctus* before rigor mortis set in.

Now one of the peculiarities of this well loved work is that, with the exception of the first and last lines, no one has the faintest idea of the words. There are maybe a few chapel organists, and the odd theology student who have a working knowledge of it, but the rest indulge in a sort of self-conscious gobbledegook. *Alleluja* and *Alabama* are the usual infills. Imagine my astonishment therefore when I perceived the lone English chorister singing the entire thing with aggressive certainty – in sharp contrast to the square-mouthed frauds sitting around him.

My admiration for this remarkable individual knew no bounds. I made it my business to seek him out on the bus journey home. I found him already seated and about to commence an in-depth study of a lurid magazine.

'You are,' I began, breaking into his concentration, 'one of the elite band of men able to sing *Sanctus* from start to finish. In addition, you are able to handle the Welsh language items in our repertoire without physical suffering. May I enquire how it is possible for an Englishman like yourself, born without the specially strengthened throat muscles of the native *Cymro* to have acquired such mastery?'

He took some time answering my question. Either I had touched a nerve, or the vividly illustrated 'Evening With Yvonne' had stultified his thought processes.

'Diligence' he replied at length, 'dedication, strength of character and the application of phonetic comparisons.'

The fellow was obviously playing a game with me.

'I'm sorry, I don't follow,' I said.

He closed the magazine with some reluctance and shot me what might be called a sidelong glance.

'To a man in my position, phonetic comparisons are literally a matter of life and death; to venture any of the Welsh hymns without their assistance would be like attempting the high jump in gumboots. Take the first two lines of the Welsh National Anthem for example. It's a totally daunting prospect for any non-Welshman, until he recognises the phonetic similarity between *Mae Hen* and *fy nhadau* and "my hen" and "haddock". Thus two practically unpronounceable lines become 'My Hen laid a haddock on top of a tree'. Phonetic comparison you see? Another excellent reference can be found in *Llef – O Iesu Mawr, rho d'anian bur* – translates naturally into, 'Oh yes it's now gone half past three'.

'The method permits the widest application, any language can be reconstituted in this simple way and, providing restraint is exercised, the results are perfectly harmonious and acceptable.'

'German also?'

'But of course.'

'What about: *Aus der Traube in die Tonne, Aus der tonne in das fass*"?'

'Quite simple- 'Wash your trousers Jimmy Connor, Wash your combs out in the bath.'

'So in other words you weren't singing *Sanctus* at all?'

'Certainly not, old chap, far too risky, certain lockjaw.'

'Phonetic comparatives?'

'Precisely.'

I felt privileged even to sit beside such an outstanding human being. I leaned forward.

'Speaking for myself, I was taught *Sanctus* at my mother's knee. Word perfect, naturally. However, I have a friend in the same section of the choir, excellent chap you understand, but a little retarded so to speak. If you would be kind enough to let me have your particular version, I'm sure it would help him enormously.'

'With the greatest of pleasure,' he said, rapidly filling

the back of an envelope with his adaption of the noble old barnstormer, and here it is, with the original Welsh version for those who still have their own teeth.

Glân geriwbiaid a seraffiaid,	Half Peruvian is Sir Alfred
Fyrdd o gylch yr orsedd fry,	Filthy rich old sot is he
Mewn olynol seiniau dibaid,	Spends his time refining Khifa
Canant fawl eu Harglwydd cu:	Canabis and L.S.D.
Llawn yw'r nefoedd o'th ogoniant,	Round his neighbours rose ebullient
Llawn yw'r ddaear, dir a môr;	Bade him lie and sin no more
Rhodder iti fythol foliant	Roared that sleazy octogoniant
Sanctaidd Sanctaidd	Shan't I, Shan't I,
Sanctaidd Iôr!	Shan't I though!

Thoughts following a concert at a Cathedral

The embargo on audience applause, encountered by choirs and musicians alike, at music concerts in some Church of England premises is one of the more inexplicable traditions of the institution. Performing before an officially muted audience is about as ineffective as chatting to someone under anaesthetic. Having tried and failed to obtain a satisfactory explanation, R.G. Mainwaring invented one:

Thus spake the Rural Dean

My Brethren in this house of God,
We gather here tonight
To listen to the 'Doonvent Choir'
(I hope I got that right).
But will you kindly not applaud
Until the concert's done;

It's much more gracious, and you'll find
That silence can be fun.
The point was made by Bishop Strong, when visiting
the town,
There's nothing so uplifting as a Christian looking down.

I think perhaps I need to stress
The message from a cross,
Though one of inspiration
Is also one of loss.
Applause is thus distasteful
When one's thoughts are of the grave
It also plays Old Harry
With the plaster in the nave.
So nod your heads to show you've heard, and wear a
little frown.
There's nothing so uplifting as a Christian looking down.

A man who serves the church as I
Never ever smiles.
He must look debilitated
As if suffering from Piles.
He must clasp his hands devoutly
And stare bleakly at his toes.
He must spread an air of lamentation
Everywhere he goes;
And that is why we priests must don this black
sepulchral gown.
There's nothing so uplifting as a Christian looking down.

At home of course a priest may prove
A man of common clay,

With six or seven children
And another on the way.
But when he dons canonicals
His thoughts must come to heel,
For 'rumpo' is but candy-floss
It's misery's for real.
I made this plain to Joshua (he's my curate,

                              Reverend Brown),
There's nothing so uplifting as a Christian looking down.

These music concerts, I'm afraid
Mean nothing much to me;
A harrowing funeral service
Is more my cup of tea.
I love those muffled moans and sobs;
When mourners try to sing
I think about my overdraft
To get into the swing.
I feel ennobled and refreshed; I seem to wear a crown.
Oh there's nothing so uplifting,
So spiritually gear shifting,
So sin and conscience sifting
As a Christian looking down.

A conversation over the garden wall

Ianto	Hello. I hear that you have been made a life member of Dunvant Male Choir.
Fred	Yes, and I am very proud of it.
Ianto	Do you think it's possible for me to join the choir?
Fred	Yes, by all means if you can sing.
Ianto	But I expect that I'd have to fill up a lot of forms?

Fred	Oh no!
Ianto	What have I got to do then?
Fred	You'll have to attend practices and at the end you will be asked to take a voice test, which will be given by the Musical Director.
Ianto	What's that for?
Fred	So that Arwyn Walters, the Conductor, can hear your voice and decide where best to put you. Either with the top tenors, second tenors, first bass, bottom bass, (or not at all of course).
Ianto	Oh Dear! If I pass, when will I get my uniform and sing in a concert?
Fred	You'll have to pass another voice test before you receive your uniform and sing in a concert.
Ianto	Why is that then? Is it like an MOT? My father says that MOTs are the mother of trouble.
Fred	If you pass your MOT, then you are required to pay your membership fee.
Ianto	How much is that going to cost me?
Fred	£20 annually, to be paid promptly in January and you are expected to attend practice twice a week. These are held at Gowerton on Tuesday and Friday evenings. When a chorister becomes an OAP, then the membership is halved.
Ianto	So I have to produce a birth certificate to prove my age?
Fred	Oh no, they'll take your word.
Ianto	I suppose that the choir members are made up from all walks of life?
Fred	Butchers, bakers, candlestick makers, painters, decorators, teachers, doctors, and, believe it or not, even retired policemen!

Ianto	So they maintain law and order for you then?
Fred	No, it's the other way round – we keep them in order. Can you read music?
Ianto	No, to be truthful, I can't read anything!
Fred	Well, that is a set back, but can you read the alphabet?
Ianto	I'm sorry: I don't go to church. I am not a religious man.
Fred	Well, not to worry. We have a system, which is known as tonic sol- fa.
Ianto	Hang on, my Dad read an advert in a newspaper. 'What do you think of this Ianto?' he said. 'Tonic sol-fa cures constipation'.
Fred	It's the other way round. It gives you constipation. Well, Ianto, I've given you the 'gen'. How old are you?
Ianto	I'll be seventy a fortnight today.
Fred	We have several members who are seventy odd in the choir. Will you think about it?
Ianto	Yes I will, but I'll have to ask my Dad.

Acknowledgements

W.B. Ellis: Côr Meibion Cwm Garw

J.G. Evans: Côr Meibion Aber (The Aber Valley Male
                                   Voice Choir)

R. Hughes: Côr Meibion Maesteg a'r Cylch (Maesteg
                                   and District Male Voice Choir)

M. Mason: Côr Meibion Llanelli (Llanelli Male Choir)

B. Morris: Côr Meibion Hwlffordd (Haverfordwest
                                   Male Voice Choir)

W. Price: Côr Meibion Pontarddulais.

M. Thomas: Côr Meibion Dowlais (Dowlais Male Choir)

A.Tucker: Côr Meibion Dyfnant (Dunvant Male Choir)

I. Watkins: Côr Meibion Caldicot (Caldicot Male
                                   Voice Choir)

Bibliography

Blwyddiadur y Methodistiaid Calfinaidd 1946

Brierley and Hiscock, *The Christian Handbook*, 1994/95

Brierley and Langley, *The Christian Handbook*, 1992/93

Congregational Year Book 1936

Cowan, W., *The Humerous Side of the Pulpit*, 1913

Dodd, C.H., *Parables of the Kingdom*

Evans, J.G., *Celebration*

Evans, I. and Jackson, P., *Bread of Heaven*, 1995

Hughes, C., Jenour, M., Braun, C., *Pass the Port*, 1976

Hughes, J.R., *Humour Sanctified*, 1902

Humphreys, C., *Buddhism*, 1949

John, Barry, *Book of Rugby*, 1973

Keating, F., *Up and Under*, 1988

Koestler, A., *Act of Creation*, 1947

Lloyd, D.M. and Lloyd, E.M. [editors], *A Book of Wales*, 1964, Collins, London and Glasgow, Pages 243-244, Daniel Owen 1836-95: 'Rhys Lewis'; Pages 287-288, Sir Henry Jones 1852-1922, 'Old Memories'; Page 271, Lloyd George's Recruiting Speech at Bangor 1915

Thomas, Dylan, *Miscellany One*, 1965, Aldine Paperbacks, Dent and Sons, Extract from 'Return Journey', pp114-5

Williams, G., Richards, H., Stead, P., *Heart and Soul: The Character of Welsh Rugby*, 1998

Y Drysorfa, 1946